Hideko S. Kunii

Graph Data Model
and Its Data Language

Foreword by Gio Wiederhold

With 35 Figures

Springer-Verlag Tokyo Berlin Heidelberg New York
London Paris Hong Kong

HIDEKO S. KUNII
General Manager
Software Division
Ricoh Co., Ltd.
Tokyo, Japan

Library of Congress Cataloging-in-Publication Data

Kunii, Hideko S., 1947–
Graph data model and its data language/Hideko S. Kunii. p.   cm. Includes biblio-
graphical references.
ISBN-13: 978-4-431-68116-8   e-ISBN-13: 978-4-431-68114-4
DOI: 10.1007/ 978-4-431-68114-4
                                        1. Data base management. 2. Data
structures (Computer science) 3. Programming languages (Electronic computers)
I. Title. QA76.9.D3K86 1990 005.74—dc20

© Springer-Verlag Tokyo 1990
Softcover reprint of the hardcover 1st edition 1990

Typesetting: Macmillan India Ltd., Bangalore

To Tosiyasu L. Kunii

Foreword

The work presented in this book is an important building block in the development of new generation of database management systems. The first generation of database management systems, IDS, IMS, TOTAL, and their derivatives (especially the CODASYL family) had to focus on efficiency by limiting themselves to rigid application semantics with predefined access paths. The second, relational generation, rejects the use of application semantics in order to achieve a great deal of flexibility.

The new generation uses high-level semantics, as defined informally in the Entity-Relationship (E-R) models, to overcome the burden that the relational model imposes on the end-user. Knowledge about the application domains is now encoded, using any of a number of formalizations of the E-R model.

This book complements the semantic approach. By providing high-level access path definitions and a full set of operations to exploit them, a model is provided to the system implementor and application designer.

High-level semantics can now be translated into an operational environment and precisely specified. Since the links which are used to compose access paths can be dynamically specified, flexibility (absent in early systems using physical links) is retained.

These operational specifications generate benefits lacking in relationally based implementations. Recursion and its closure can be established, ordering of records can be defined, and indexes can be required. Record lists, consisting only of record-identifiers, provide a useful intermediate structure so that materialization of large record sets can be avoided. Storage primitives are also made explicit, so that update, as well as, query is formalized.

In summary, this book contributes an important foundation for the implementation of new database management systems which free the end-user from having to know and specify inter-relational semantics, and provide results flexibly and efficiently. It should be studied by anyone contemplating an implementation of a modern database management system.

GIO WIEDERHOLD
Professor
Department of Computer Science
Stanford University

Preface

The environments in which database management systems (DBMSs) are being used or needed have changed rapidly in the last several years with the advance of hardware technology. There are two major changes that are very relevant to this book. One is the diversity of data types in database applications that cannot be easily expressed in the form of tables. That is, today's advanced applications often involve image and graphics data as well as conventional text data. The other is the availability of graphical user interfaces, which is becoming one of the standard facilities in UNIX[1] workstations.

Although the relational model originated by E. F. Codd has made prominent contribution in the research on database systems, recent database applications are outgrowing this model. The table-based model, i.e., the relational model, is not the best approach to express complex and diverse databases. Contemporary advanced graphical user interfaces have made a graph-oriented approach described in this book feasible and attractive.

The concepts of Graph Data Model (GDM) and its data language, Graph Data Language (GDL), provide an alternative to the relational approach, serving as a framework of the DBMSs that satisfy the needs of today's database applications. The GDM can be classified as a binary data model; therefore, it has some correspondence with the Entity–Relationship model (E–R model) originated by P. P. S. Chen. The major difference between these two models lies in the level of data representations and data operations. The E–R model deals with the semantics of databases while the GDM deals with only the structure of databases.

The work of the GDM/GDL has a rather long history. I started it in 1979 at The University of Texas at Austin where I earned my doctorate in computer sciences. In 1982 I joined Ricoh Co., Ltd., and since then this work has been continued in the DBMS laboratory, Software Research Center, Ricoh Co., Ltd. Up to now, two DBMSs have been implemented in this laboratory. The recent one runs on several UNIX

---

[1] UNIX is a registered trademark of AT&T.

machines such as Sun[2] Workstation and VAX[3], and is commercially available from Ricoh Co., Ltd. This software package product is called **G-BASE** in Japan and **RICOHBASE** in other countries. The current version of G-BASE (RICOHBASE) has implemented most of the concepts of GDM/GDL except some link operators.

When I first proposed the GDM/GDL in the early 1980s, computer hardware was not ready to accommodate graphical user interfaces. Today, the situation has changed drastically. Most of the popular hardware and software display graphical capabilities for increased visuality. I believe that the concepts of GDM/GDL provide, in terms of the graph structure, a very firm and clear framework for new generation DBMSs needed today.

To summarize the book, it defines and describes the Graph Data Language, sketches the implementation of a database management system based on this language, and compares the performance characteristics of this system with relational database management systems.

The GDL is proposed to be a high-level data language which allows execution efficiency without losing data independence and which can be compactly implemented. GDL is founded on graphs and an algebra which operates on graphs. The GDM is the framework for GDL. The GDM formulates schemas as directed graphs and data operations as algebraic operations on these graphs. The nodes of a schema graph represent record types; the arcs of the graph represent link types that are treated as logical access paths. A link type is a representation of a many-to-many relationship between two record types. I developed link operators which endow GDL with high expressive power including explicit representations of numerical quantifiers, irreflexive transitive closure and grouping. GDL also allows recursive link types that represent relationships within a single record type.

The facilities of GDL are carried by two components: the DDL (Data Definition Language) and the DML (Data Manipulation Language). The DDL implements definition of schemas and views, both of which may contain integrity constraints. The DML provides a set-at-a-time query interface (in the sense that a set of qualified occurrences is retrieved at a time by a single DML statement) as well as a procedural interface. A query is expressed as a path on a connected graph. Record types on a path may be recursively qualified by other paths. This approach gives the system the necessary guidance for determining access paths, thus reducing execution overhead of the GDM-based database management system.

GDL allows dynamic creation and deletion of link types. Because of this feature, the restriction that queries are represented as a path on a

---

[2]Sun is a registered trademark of Sun Microsystems, Inc.
[3]VAX is a registered trademark of Digital Equipment Corporation.

connected graph does not limit the power of the language. It also supports data independence since the user can redefine record types and links as a schema evolves.

I have given here a prototype implementation design of a GDM/GDL-based system. The GDL concepts are shown to correspond closely to implementation concepts. Performance of access path strategies was compared between GDM and the relational model by using an extension of Yao's cost model. The GDM based system was found to yield excellent performance for queries where a small number of occurrences are qualified by the queries and for queries that contain semi-joins.

HIDEKO S. KUNII

Acknowledgments

During the course of this research, I have received assistance from many people. I would particularly like to thank Prof. J. C. Browne, who served as my dissertation advisor, for his guidance, valuable comments, and encouragement. I am also grateful to Dr. U. Dayal, Prof. A. Dale, Prof. M. Malek, Prof. M. Gouda, Prof. G. Wiederhold, Mr. K. Kanasaki, and Prof. K. Yamaguchi for their helpful remarks.

Ricoh Company, Ltd. allowed me to complete this book. I especially thank Mr. H. Hamada, Mr. T. Nawate, and Mr. K. Kubo for their understanding.

I am greatly indebted to my husband, Tosiyasu L. Kunii, and son, Michiaki, for their patience and encouragement.

Author

Table of Contents

1. Introduction

1.1 Motivation

A data language is a language for defining and manipulating databases. The framework for a data language is a data model; that is, the formal abstract definition of the data objects and relationships together with the operations on the structures supported in the data language. A data language consists of a data definition language (DDL) that defines the data objects and relationships, and a data manipulation language (DML) that expresses operations on the objects defined in the DDL.

Significant desirable characteristics of a data language include:

- Representational power of the data organization (objects and relationships) defined in the DDL
- Computational power of the operation set defined in the DML
- Ease of application including initial formulation, programming and modification
- Execution efficiency
- Compactness of the system

The relative importance of each of these characteristics varies strongly between applications.

This list of application-oriented characteristics can be mapped to a set of requirements for a data language:

- Support by the data model for formal definition of both data structures and operations on the data structures
- Support for a high-level query representation
- Data independence, in the sense that logical data structures are decoupled from physical data structuring
- Ready mapping of logical data structures to physical structures on contemporary computer architectures

This book defines and characterizes a data language that occupies a unique position with respect to this list of requirements.

Research [3, 13, 72, 69, 76, 82, 24, 8, 80] aimed at development of data languages which meet these requirements has been founded mostly on the relational data model originated by E. F. Codd [19]. The relational model achieves:

- Data independence, in the sense that the evolution of data organization and the evolution of manipulation programs do not interfere with each other
- A formal abstract definition of data organization and manipulation
- A non-procedural query representation

Data independence reduces the maintenance work of data and programs; the second and third features simplify query representation and enhance the representational power of the data language. The simple formal definition of the relational model has motivated extensive theoretical and experimental research.

Data language systems based on the relational model have had serious deficiencies with respect to a few of the significant desirable characteristics and/or requirements listed previously. Firstly, it is not straightforward to obtain efficiency in execution. In the relational model, relationships among relations (records) are not structurally specified. A user interprets the values of certain pairs of attributes as indicating or representating relationships. (Let us call this value-based representation of relationships.) Conventional computer architecture does not, however, directly support access to records by values. Actual implementations of the relational model may provide access paths for improving execution efficiency, as in System R [3]. Translation from a value-based query representation into an optimal execution sequence of basic operations utilizing appropriate access paths can, however, be very complex. (Chapter 6 will discuss the performance of various access-path strategies.) Secondly, the relational model is basically a set of tables. Such a flat structure is not helpful to a user attempting to comprehend the logical structure actually existing in a schema. A more structured data organization is suitable and natural for some applications. Thirdly, the expressive power of the relational model is not sufficient to formulate arbitrary and complex queries in a non-procedural or set-at-a-time manner. The *set-at-a-time* manner means that a single DML statement can retrieve a set of qualified occurrences at a time while only a single occurrence is retrieved at a time in a *record-at-a-time* manner. Queries involving transitive closure or numerical quantifiers are often encountered, for example, in graphics applications.

Value-based representations of relationships among relations (records) do not give the database management system (DBMS) guidance for the formulation of efficient query processing. It is difficult for a user to estimate execution costs and probable response times of complex queries because they depend upon the algorithms used in query processing. There have been extensive efforts to improve execution efficiency of the relational model [3, 80, 62, 14]. Database machines [56, 5] designed to process relational type queries efficiently have been proposed and indeed implemented [31].

An essential element of the relational approach is the complete removal of the task of access path specification from the user. This often simplifies query formulation; but it imposes a heavy burden on the system to determine access paths. This is our point of departure for seeking a data language that preserves the advantages of the relational model but that does not retain its disadvantages. We require the user to describe his or her access paths at a *logical level*. That is, the logical access paths between two record types are represented by links. The concept of link is not at all new. The novelty of our approach is the development of an algebraic treatment of links, set-at-a-time query representation in terms of the properties of links, and link-oriented query computations. Our goal is to design a data model based on a graph structure which retains the desirable properties that the relational model achieved and simultaneously overcomes the performance and provides structural representation of databases.

1.2 Overview

This research attempts the formulation and analysis of a data model and a data language which meets the requirements mentioned previously. We particularly aim at a formal definitional structure, a set-at-a-time query representation, reasonable cost of execution and data independence. As an alternative approach to the relational one, we propose a *Graph Data Model* (GDM) and a *Graph Data Language* (GDL) which is founded on GDM. The data structure of GDM is a labelled directed graph. *Records* are represented as nodes characterized by attributes and holding values. *Links*, which are interpreted as binary relationships between records, are represented by directed arcs. Links serve as logical access paths. GDL is based upon algebraic operations on the graphs. We have investigated the semantics of links and developed powerful link operators. The concept of *record list*, which integrates records and links into a single object, is introduced to retain intermediate results of computations.

GDL consists of a data definition language (DDL) and a data manipulation language (DML). DDL provides facilities for defining and changing schemas and views. These definitions may include integrity constraints. The definitions of constraints and views are operational; that is, the language constructs in the DML are also used to define constraints and views. DML provides facilities for manipulating both records and links. The DML and DDL are integrated, in that dynamic definition of both records and links is supported. The strategies taken in the design of GDL are:

- Users are given the ability to structure query processing.
- Queries are represented in terms of graph traversals.
- The query language interface is a structured non-procedural language using extended path expressions.
- Dynamic (execution time) specification of logical access paths and record definitions is supported.

A user of this system can, by specifying logical access paths (links), give the system guidance for the development of efficient processing structures for the queries a user *expects* to perform. The user has control over crucial performance factors which only he or she can know, by specifying information which is a property only of a *logical structure* of the application and not the physical representations used by the DBMS to represent these logical features. This approach, together with the rule in DML that a query must be expressed as a connected graph, improves performance without complex optimizations and avoids disastrous performances on complex queries. Of course, it is not desirable to force a user to know or understand the details of physical storage access paths. The access paths defined in GDL are logical access paths meaningful to the user rather than physical access paths. They are, however, readily mappable to executable representations on conventional architecture.

The data model further incorporates the capability of creating and deleting record types and link types dynamically, to support the evolution of schemas. We can in this way achieve *practical* data independence. Users, as their requirements change, can dynamically change data organization to conform to changes in application requirements. A separate data reorganization language is, therefore, not needed in GDL.

The DML of GDL has advantages over a data language based on the relational calculus or relational algebra, in addition to ease in obtaining low-cost execution. The algebraic basis of GDL has added power over that of relational algebra. The algebra based on GDM can directly express transitive closure, numerical quantifiers and grouping. (Higher level languages based on relational algebra or calculus can of course be extended to include these features as demonstrated by the transitive closure in QBE [82].)

This book is divided into seven chapters. The rest of this chapter discusses previous work related to our research. Chapter 2 contains the definition of GDM. The data definition facility and data manipulation facility of GDL are described in Chapter 3 and Chapter 4, respectively. Chapter 5 outlines a prototype implementation of GDL. In Chapter 6 we compare GDM with the relational model with respect to performance of access path strategies. Chapter 7 concludes by assessing the contribution of this research to the field and discussing future research.

1.3 Related Work

Many high-level query languages or formal frameworks for network-oriented data models have been proposed. Some of these languages are specifically designed for the CODASYL network structure [11, 54]. Some are proposed for heterogeneous data models in order to integrate hierarchical, network and relational models [25, 44]. Others are designed for data models which formulate a database as some type of graph, such as the Entity-Relationship model [17] and the functional model [30, 64]. This section discusses these languages and formalizations, and elucidates the differences and relationships between them and GDL.

The Link and Selector Language (LSL) proposed by D. Tsichritzis [72] has a similar approach to GDL in the sense that LSL also intends to solve performance problems by making access paths visible. LSL allows, however, only one primitive type of operation on links. The representational power of LSL is a subset of that of GDL.

An extended owner-coupled set data model proposed by J. Bradley [11] developed a non-procedural language on a CODASYL-like graph data structure. It is, however, a restrictive data model because linkages between record types are allowed only if corresponding connection fields exist in those record types. This type of linkage is similar to virtual link types of GDL described in Chap. 2. Manola and Pirotte [54] also designed a high-level query language, CQLF, for CODASYL-type databases. CQLF is similar to non-procedural languages in the relational model such as SQL [13] and QUEL [69]. The implementation of these non-procedural languages will, however, like the relational model, face the problem of finding optimal query processing. The designers of these languages have not developed tactics to overcome this problem. (Note that Dayal and Goodman investigated this problem [26].)

NQUEL, proposed by U. Dayal [24, 25], is a non-procedural data language for a generalized network model. We adopt NQUEL-like notation for link operators in GDL. The approach taken in NQUEL is very different from GDL. That is, NQUEL treats links merely as logical relationships while GDL treats links as logical access paths. NQUEL is based on predicate calculus, while GDL is algebraic, i.e., queries are constructed by composing elementary operations. GDL offers an expanded set of operations on links, to enable query processing of GDL. Computational power is increased in GDL. Jacobs [44] proposed database logic as a framework for a DML for heterogeneous databases including the relational, hierarchical and network models. It is an application of mathematical logic to databases.

The Unified Database Language (UDL) proposed by C. J. Date [22] is claimed to accommodate both record-at-a-time and set-at-a-time manipulations on network data structures which are more abstract than the CODASYL data structure. (Relational and hierarchical data models are treated as subsets of the network model.) Record-at-a-time manipulations are made clear in UDL by the use of a "cursor" concept. Manipulations on the network structure are rather navigational, like the CODASYL network model. For example, a nested access path structure cannot be expressed by a single DML statement. Therefore, set-at-a-time manipulations on the network structure are not fully supported in UDL.

DAPLEX, proposed by Shipman [64], is a data language based on a functional data model. The basic concepts of this model are the entity and the function. Entities and functions of a schema are represented by nodes and arcs, respectively, in a graph. DAPLEX is a procedural language. Basic algebraic operations are not formally defined.

The path expressions in a language designed by Schneiderman and Thomas [65] to describe database conversion, can be thought of as a degenerate case of the path expressions in GDL. Their underlying data structure is a CODASYL-like network model. Path expressions are also used in GORDAS, designed by Elmasri and Wiederhold [30]. GORDAS is a formal high-level language for the Entity-Relationship model. These path expressions do not contain the concept of operations on both links and nested structures of path expressions.

In comparison with these languages, the data structure of GDL is not restricted to a CODASYL-type network structure; it is a generalized network structure (graph). Operations on the network structure are formally defined. Records and links are not associated with particular semantics, unlike the Entity-Relationship model and the DAPLEX functional model. Rather, they are operational objects in GDL. Links are treated as logical access paths, as in LSL, and GDL provides extended operations on the links. Its DML is algebraic. GDL provides a powerful set of algebraic operations for defining networks in terms of other networks. These operations can be used to retrieve networks (records and links), and to create network views or change the schema dynamically. Most of the other languages provide mechanisms only for retrieving "flat" records. (NQUEL is an exception because it does have statements for defining network views.)

2. Graph Data Model

2.1 Overview

This chapter describes the Graph Data Model (GDM) that underlies the GDL Data Definition and Data Manipulation Languages. A schema is represented by a labeled directed graph whose nodes represent records and whose arcs represent links. A query is formulated as an *algebraic expression* on the graph. Our data language to express queries is called an *Elementary Data Language*. The operations on the graph are called *Elementary Data Operations*, and these include manipulations of both records and links. The semantics of links are incorporated into the data model as definitions of link operators. Relationships among records are represented directly by the properties of linkage. It will be shown that a link-based data language is at least as powerful as a value-based data language.

At query-processing time, records and links are unified into a single object, called a record list, which is a list of records. A link can be thought of as a binary record list, while a record is a unary record list. The record list is also considered as an abstraction of a two-level hierarchy of records and their values. The Elementary Data Operations of GDM are defined on the record lists.

The computational power of our Graph Data Model is greater than that of the relational calculus and algebra [19]. Link operators, which include the operations defined in the relational algebra and also extend to include transitive closure and numerical quantifiers (including existential and universal quantifiers), have been defined. Link operations are often more efficiently executed on conventional computers than value-based operations if the number of occurrences retrieved is small.

2.2 Schema

A *schema*, denoted by S, is a logical description of a database. It consists of a set of record types, $\underline{R}$, and a set of link types, $\underline{L}$:

$$S = (\underline{R}, \underline{L})$$

$\underline{L}$ can be an empty set. Let R_i and L_j denote a record type and a link type, respectively. $\underline{R}$ and $\underline{L}$ are expressed as:

$$\underline{R} = \{R_i : i = 1, \ldots, m\} \quad \text{and} \quad \underline{L} = \{L_j : j = 1, \ldots, n\}$$

where m is the number of record types in S, and n is the number of link types in S. A schema can be represented as a graph whose nodes represent record types, and whose arcs represent link types.

Associated with each record type R_i is an ordered set (a list) of attributes, $\underline{A}_i$. We write it as:

$$\underline{A}_i = (A_{i1}, A_{i2}, \ldots, A_{if_i})$$

Each attribute A_{ik} in $\underline{A}_i$ is associated with a domain of its values, $domain\,(A_{ik})$. Let V_{ik} denote a value of A_{ik}. An occurrence r_i of a given record type R_i is expressed as:

$$r_i = (V_{i1}, V_{i2}, \ldots, V_{if_i})$$

f_i denotes the number of attributes in R_i. The attributes are *compatible* if they are defined on the same domain.

A link type represents a binary relationship of record types. A link type L_j is defined by an ordered pair of record types:

$$L_j = (R_i, R_{i'}), \quad L_j \in \underline{L}, \quad R_i, R_{i'} \in \underline{R}$$

An occurrence l_j of a given link type L_j is expressed as:

$$l_j = (r_i, r_{i'}) \text{ where } r_i \in R_i \text{ and } r_{i'} \in R_{i'}$$

The following terms are used with respect to L_j:

1. L_j is *incident* with R_i and $R_{i'}$.
2. R_i and $R_{i'}$ are the *endpoints* of L_j.
3. R_i is the *initial node (record type)* of L_j.
4. $R_{i'}$ is the *terminal node (record type)* of L_j.

We allow a self-loop link type that links a record type to itself, i.e., $L_j = (R_i, R_i)$. We call this kind of link type a *recursive link type*. *Ordering* within a record type can be expressed by a recursive link type. The Graph Data Model allows a schema to contain more than one link type having the identical pair of an initial and a terminal node, for example,

$$L_j = (R_i, R_{i'}) \quad \text{and} \quad L_{j'} = (R_i, R_{i'})$$

where

$$L_j \neq L_{j'}.$$

We say that L_j and $L_{j'}$ are *parallel*. Hence, a schema is a general directed graph. (A directed multigraph has the second property. Together with the first property, viz self-loops, it becomes a general directed graph.) Because of the existence of parallel link types, we explicitly specify the link types used in a traversal of a schema.

Unlike the CODASYL DBTG network model [27], links are *not restricted* to being inverse functions (i.e., $1:n$). Such a restriction can, however, be defined as an integrity constraint on a schema.

A *state* (or extension), denoted as $\$S$, of a given schema S is determined by actual occurrences of record types and link types. Let $\$R_i$ and $\$L_j$ denote a state of R_i and a state of L_j, respectively. Then, $\$S$ is expressed as:

$$S = (\$\underline{R}, \$\underline{L})$$

where
$$\$\underline{R} = \{\$R_i : i = 1, \ldots, m\}$$

$$\$\underline{L} = \{\$L_j : j = 1, \ldots, n\}$$

Further, we write:

$$\$R_i = \{r_i : r_i \in R_i \wedge (r_i \text{ is stored in the database for } R_i)\}$$

and
$$\$L_j = \{l_j : l_j \in L_j \wedge (l_j \text{ is stored in the database for } L_j)\}$$

The number of distinct occurrences of a given type is called the *cardinality* of the type. Note that the existence of a link occurrence requires the existence of its initial and terminal node record occurrences. A *type* is an abstraction of a set of occurrences of the same property. The state of a given type refers to the set of occurrences for the type at a given time. The results of Elementary Data Operations are defined against the state of a schema. Permissible states of a schema may be restricted by integrity constraints which will be described in Chap. 3.

For a given link type L, we define an *inverse link type* denoted by $\%L$ as a link type which has, except direction, the same structure as L and the inverse occurrences:

$$\$(\%L) = \{(r_2, r_1) : (r_1, r_2) \in \$L\}$$

The other notations that will be used to describe the Elementary Data Operations are as follows. Suppose $X = (A_{i1}, A_{i2}, \ldots, A_{ip}) \subseteq \underline{A}_i$. Let r denote an occurrence of a record type R, then:

1. *domain* (X) is the Cartesian product of *domain* (A_{ik}), $k = 1, \ldots, p$.
2. $r[X]$ is the value of r on domain (X).
3. $R[X] = \{r[X] : r \in R\}$.

2.3 Elementary Data Operations

GDM Elementary Data Operations are operations on the schema described in the previous section. A DML statement can be translated into a sequence of elementary data operations. They are classified into:

– Set operations
– Database operations

The set operations of GDL are union ($+$), intersection ($\cap$), and difference ($-$). Since these operations have their conventional definitions, we do not discuss them further. The database operations are *restriction, record list projection, projection, link creation,* two basic types of *link traversal operations* and four types of *storage operations*. To describe these operations, we first introduce the concept of record list as a transient object for query processing.

2.3.1 Record List

A *record list* is a transient object that unifies records and links and is created at query-processing time. A record list type *RL* is an ordered set of record types:

$$RL = \langle E_1, E_2, \ldots, E_n \rangle$$

E_i is associated with $R_i \in \underline{R}$. Two different record types E_i and E_j, where $i \neq j$, can be associated with the same record type $R_i \in \underline{R}$.

Definition 1: $\underline{E}_{RL} = \{E_1, E_2, \ldots, E_n\}$

Definition 2: n is the degree of *RL*

A record list *rl* is an occurrence of a record list type *RL*. It is written as:

$$rl = (r_1, r_2, \ldots, r_n)$$

where $r_i \in R_i$

Definition 3: $rl[E_i] = r_i$

Definition 4: $rl[E_i \cdot A_{ik}] = r_i[A_{ik}]$

We introduce this concept of record list for the following reason. It is often possible to avoid making access to record occurrences when processing a query. That is, if some access path is available, it is not always necessary to obtain values for records in the path in order to evaluate a query. To keep the intermediate results, however, we must be able to retain the information that uniquely identifies the resultant record occurrences. A record list is such a facility. We can also avoid concatenating record occurrences until it is actually necessary.

A record list is an abstraction of a two-level hierarchy: it is a list of unique record identifiers and the values of attributes underneath them. Query evaluation proceeds primarily at the first level. When a database operation needs values of attributes, it descends to the second level, coming back to the first level before it goes to the next operation. The passing of information between two database operations is done at a record list level. Attributes are hidden under elements of record lists.

2.3.2 Restriction

A restriction operation (RST) selects the occurrences of a record list type that satisfy a given qualification. It is similar to the restriction operation defined in the relational algebra. A difference is that a GDM restriction is extended to operate on a record list type *RL* rather than on a single record type. A restriction is denoted by *RL*[P] where P is a predicate for the restriction. Formally it is defined as:

$$RL[P] = \{rl : rl \in RL \wedge P\ (rl)\}$$

A restriction involves either one or two attributes. The designation of an attribute needs not only the name of the attribute, A_{ik}, but also the name of the record type, E_i, of which A_{ik} is an attribute. The restriction can be a comparison of an attribute and a value, or a comparison of two attributes which can be of different record types:

1. $E_i \cdot A_{ik}$ ⟨c-op⟩ value
2. $E_i \cdot A_{ik}$ ⟨c-op⟩ $E_{i'} \cdot A_{i'k'}$

⟨c-op⟩ is one of the following:

$$=, \neq, <, \leq, > \text{ and } \geq.$$

i' can be the same as i. $P(rl)$ is, however, not a join predicate as it is in the relational algebra, even if $i \neq i'$. This is because rl is created as the result of some link traversal(s). This type of restriction can be executed only after the record types are joined by link operators. Corresponding to each format, $P(rl)$ is true if and only if:

1. $rl[E_i \cdot A_{ik}]$ ⟨c-op⟩ value
2. $rl[E_i \cdot A_{ik}]$ ⟨c-op⟩ $rl[E_{i'} \cdot A_{i'k'}]$

2.3.3 Record List Projection

A record list projection operation (RL_PROJ) creates a new *record list type* from another. On the other hand, a projection operation which will be defined in the next section creates a new *record type* from a record list. Record list projection is used with other operations to form a proper resultant record list type. Let EL denote the specification of how a new record list type is created from an existent record list type. We can write EL as:

$$EL = \langle E_1, E_2, \ldots, E_n \rangle$$

where $E_i \in \underline{E}_{RL}$. E_i is associated with a subset of $\underline{A}_i$ of the corresponding R_i. We define a record list projection, denoted by $RL\langle EL \rangle$, as follows:

$$RL\langle EL \rangle = \{(rl[E_1], rl[E_2], \ldots,$$
$$rl[E_n]) : rl \in RL\}$$

2.3.4 Projection

A projection operation (PROJ) creates a new record type from a given record list type. It requires a specification of how the record type is to be created from the record list type. Let EL_P be this specification. We can write EL_P as follows:

$$EL_P = (E_{p1} \cdot A_{p1q1}, E_{p2} \cdot A_{p2q2}, \ldots, E_{pl} \cdot A_{plql})$$

where $1 \leq pi \leq n$, $A_{piqi} \in \underline{A}_{pi}$ and $E_i \in \underline{E}_{RL}$. A projection operation, denoted by $RL(EL_P)$, is defined as:

$$RL(EL_P) = \{(rl[E_{p1} \cdot A_{p1q1}], rl[E_{p2} \cdot A_{p2q2}], \ldots,$$
$$rl[E_{pl} \cdot A_{plql}]) : rl \in RL\}$$

Note that a projection creates a record type while a record list projection creates a record list type.

2.3.5 Link Creation

If a query involves relationships between more than one record type, we express the relationships in terms of the properties of the link types connecting the record types. If no link type exists between two record types, we first construct a link type between them, by a link creation operation (LNKCRT). Suppose we construct a link type $L = (R_1, R_2)$. The link creation operation is denoted by $R_1[P]R_2$ where P is a predicate describing a relationship between R_1 and R_2. It is defined as:

$$R_1[P]R_2 = \{(r_1, r_2): r_1 \in R_1 \wedge r_2 \in R_2 \wedge P(r_1, r_2)\}$$

Note that we can consider R_1 and R_2 as unary record list types. Their values are not concatenated by this operation. It has the following format:

$$R_1 \cdot A_{1_k} \langle \text{c-op} \rangle R_2 \cdot A_{2_{k'}}$$

or

$$R_2 \cdot A_{2_{k'}} \langle \text{c-op} \rangle R_1 \cdot A_{1_k}$$

If P is omitted, this operation is simply a Cartesian product of R_1 and R_2.

The inverse link type $\%L$ is automatically created by the system whenever L is created. Otherwise, the system would not be able to delete efficiently a link occurrence whose terminal node had been deleted.

2.3.6 Link Operators

The Graph Data Model provides extensive link traversal operations. Because of this facility, the model can express many types of relationship between record types. There are basically two types of link operators: *numerical link operators* and *transitive link operators*. *Existential link operators* and *universal link operators* are defined as variants of numerical link operators. Since the existential link operators are very frequently used, we describe them separately from the numerical link operators. These operators are chosen so that many common queries can be expressed in a single DML statement. Complex relationships between record types, including transitive closure and numerical quantifiers, are directly expressed in terms of link operators. A link operator takes the following operands:

1. A link type, L
2. A record list type containing an initial node, RL_1
3. An initial node, R_1
4. A record list type containing a terminal node, RL_2
5. A terminal node, R_2
6. A mode specification, $MODE$
7. A comparison specification, $\langle q \rangle$ (for numerical and transitive link operators)
8. One or two grouping specifications, X_1 and X_2 (optional)

In a DML statement, not all of these need be explicitly specified by the user. RL_1, RL_2 and $MODE$ can be determined from the context. $MODE$ tells which record type(s) should be retrieved:

1. Neutral mode: both R_1 and R_2
2. Downward mode: only R_2
3. Upward mode: only R_1

The first case is allowed only when the link operator accompanies no grouping. The endpoint(s) to be retrieved is (are) called the *target*(s) of the link traversal. The semantics of link operators varies depending on the *MODE*. In the upward mode, this operation is similar to the feature of "having" in SEQUEL [3]. Note that only R_1 and R_2 actively participate in link traversal. $\langle q \rangle$ is described in Sects. 2.3.6.3 and 2.3.6.4. Grouping is described in Sect. 2.3.6.1.

Application of link operators may be complex. We decompose it into the following sequence of operations:

1. Grouping of R_1 and R_2 by X_1 and X_2, if any (GROUP)
2. Link traversal from R_1 to R_2 with L, producing *RESULT* (TRAVERSE)
3. Formation of a resultant record list type from RL_1, RL_2, R_1 and R_2 (FORM)

The GROUP operation is not applicable to a transitive link operator. Only the TRAVERSE operation differs from one link operator to another. We write a link operator as:

$$RL_1 [MODE: \text{traversal expression}] RL_2$$

Definition of traversal expressions is given in the following descriptions of link operators.

2.3.6.1 Grouping

Some queries involve properties of aggregates of link occurrences rather than properties of individual link occurrences. For example, consider the educational database shown in Fig. 2.1. A rectangle denotes a record type. An arrow denotes a link type. This schema has two record types, COURSE and ENROLLMENT, and a link type, ENROLLS. Suppose we want to find SNO of the students who took all the core courses. To express this in our Graph Data Model, we group the record occurrences of ENROLLMENT by SNO. We then test each group for whether it is linked to all the core courses.

Let x be in *domain* (X). Formally we define a *group* to be an equivalence class on R_i:

$$g_{R_i}(X, x) = \{r : r \in R_i \wedge r[X\ ] = x\}$$

Record occurrences of a record type are partitioned into disjoint groups such that the value of an occurrence of X is the same as that of every other occurrence within its group. Further, we denote the collection of these groups by:

$$G_{R_i}(X) = \{g_{R_i}(X, x) : x \in R_i[X]\}$$

After groupings are specified with link operators, the TRAVERSE operations are performed on the groups. Otherwise, they are performed on individual occurrences. The projections which appear in a query expressed in the relational algebra can be replaced by this grouping except for the projection at the end of the algebraic expression.

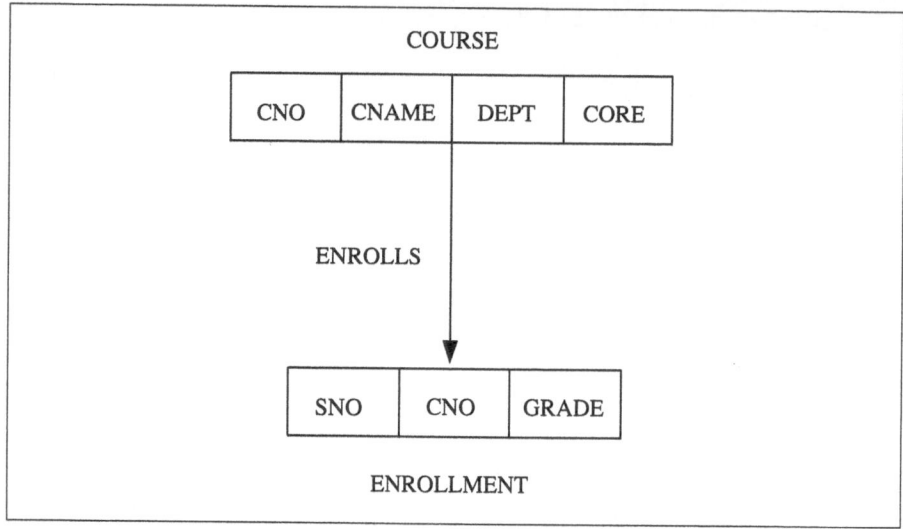

Fig. 2.1. Schema diagram of simple educational database

Grouping has been incorporated into the relational model in the form of quotient relations, and an algebra of quotient relations has been defined [34].

2.3.6.2 Existential link operators

This section and the next two sections describe the semantics of TRAVERSE operations of link operators. An existential link operator (EXT) checks existence of links between two record types, expressing an existential quantifier. This is one variant of a numerical link operator (see Sect. 2.3.6.3). The traversal expression of this link type is:

Downward mode:

$$R_1 \to /L/(X_2) \to R_2$$

Upward mode:

$$R_1 \to (X_1)/L/ \to R_2$$

Note that it is not meaningful to define grouping on both node record types. If a grouping is not involved, the existential link operator (EXT) returns:

Neutral mode:

$$\{(r_1, r_2) \quad : \quad r_1 \in R_1 \wedge r_2 \in R_2 \wedge \exists l \in L(l = (r_1, r_2))\}$$

Downward mode:

$$\{(r_2) \quad : \quad r_2 \in R_2 \wedge \exists r_1 \in R_1 \ \exists l \in L(l = (r_1, r_2))\}$$

Upward mode:

$$\{(r_1) \quad : \quad r_1 \in R_1 \wedge \exists r_2 \in R_2 \ \exists l \in L(l = (r_1, r_2))\}$$

When grouping is specified, this operation is extended to retrieve all the members of the groups, in each of which there is at least one member that is linked to at least one occurrence of the other record type. The semantics depends on the mode:

Downward mode:

$$\{(r_2) \quad : \quad r_2 \in R_2 \wedge \exists r_1 \in R_1 \, \exists r_2' \in g_{R_2}(X_2, r_2[X_2]) \, \exists l \in L(l = (r_1, r_2'))\}$$

Upward mode:

$$\{(r_1) \quad : \quad r_1 \in R_1 \wedge \exists r_2 \in R_2 \, \exists r_1' \in g_{R_1}(X_1, r_1[X_1]) \, \exists l \in L(l = (r_1', r_2))\}$$

In the case where grouping exists in an existential link operator, we allow the retrieval of only either an initial node or a terminal node. Otherwise, the occurrences of the target record type that are in one of the qualified groups, but that are not directly linked to the other node record type, would have to be paired with null values.

Let us show how this operator can be used. Consider the educational database in Fig. 2.1. In order to retrieve all the ENROLLMENTs of those students who took a database course (DB), we use the downward mode of the existential link operator. Figure 2.3 gives an expression for this retrieval. The first form is a GDL algebraic expression. The second form is a partial statement of our DML. DML statements will be described in Chap. 4. The result of the query for the state shown in Fig. 2.2 is also given in Fig. 2.3.

The negation of this link operator is called a negative existential link operator (NEGEXT). It is expressed as:

Downward mode: $R_1 \rightarrow / \, \tilde{}L/(X_2) \rightarrow R_2$

Upward mode: $R_1 \rightarrow (X_1)/ \, \tilde{}L/ \rightarrow R_2$

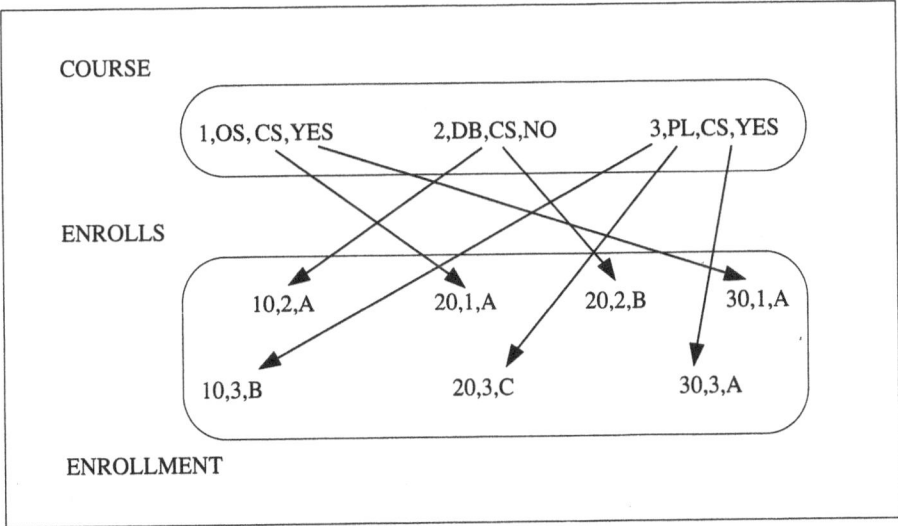

Fig. 2.2. State of simple educational database

Query 2-1:

    Retrieve all the ENROLLMENT occurrences of the students
who took DB course

Algebraic expression:

    <COURSE> [COURSE.CNAME = "DB"]
      [downward mode: COURSE → /ENROLLES/(SNO) →
    ENROLLMENT] <ENROLLMENT>
    (ENROLLMENT.SNO, ENROLLMENT.CNO,
    ENROLLMENT.GRADE)

Partial DML statement:

    COURSE [CNAME = "DB"] → /ENROLLS/(SNO) →
    ENROLLMENT

Result:

    { (10,2,A), (10,3,B), (20,1,A), (20,2,B), (20,3,C) }

Fig. 2.3. Example of existential link operator

If we denote the result of the corresponding existential link operator by *RESULT*, the semantics of the negative existential link operator can be written as:

1. Without grouping
   Neutral mode: $R_1 \times R_2 - RESULT$
   Downward mode: $R_2 - RESULT$
   Upward mode: $R_1 - RESULT$
2. With grouping
   Downward mode: $R_2 - RESULT$
   Upward mode: $R_1 - RESULT$

The $R_1 \times R_2$ denotes the Cartesian product of R_1 and R_2.

2.3.6.3 Numerical link operators

A numerical link operator (NUM) provides a user with a powerful facility to express relationships between two record types. We write the traversal expression of this operator as:

$$R_1 \rightarrow (X_1)//\langle q \rangle L//(X_2) \rightarrow R_2$$

where $\langle q \rangle$ is of the form: $\langle c\text{-op} \rangle\ n$. If the comparison operator $\langle c\text{-op} \rangle$ is omitted, "=" is assumed. The grouping is optional. It can be specified for both nodes or either node. n is either a positive integer or a symbol "+". If no grouping is involved, the numerical link operator specifies that each occurrence of a target record type must be linked to a specified number of occurrences of another record type. The symbol "+" denotes the cardinality of a given initial or terminal node. In other words, it expresses a universal quantifier. When grouping is specified, the preceding definitions are applied to the groups instead of individual occurrences. The semantics of a numerical link operator for the case where $\langle q \rangle$ is "$= n$" is defined as:

1. Without grouping
   Neutral mode:

$$\{(r_1, r_2) \ : \ r_1 \in R_1 \ \wedge \ r_2 \in R_2 (\exists n) l \in L(l = (r_1, r_2))\}$$

   Downward mode:

$$\{(r_2) \ : \ r_2 \in R_2 \ \wedge \ (\exists n) r_1 \in R_1 \ \exists l \in L(l = (r_1, r_2))\}$$

   Upward mode:

$$\{(r_1) \ : \ r_1 \in R_1 \ \wedge \ (\exists n) r_2 \in R_2 \ \exists l \in L(l = (r_1, r_2))\}$$

2. With grouping
   Downward mode:

$$\{(r_2) \ : \ r_2 \in R_2 \ \wedge \ (\exists n) g_{R_1} \in G_{R_1}(X_1) \exists r_1 \in g_{R_1} \exists r_2' \in g_{R_2}(X_2, r_2[X_2])$$
$$\exists l \in L(l = (r_1, r_2'))\}$$

   Upward mode:

$$\{(r_1) \ : \ r_1 \in R_1 \ \wedge \ (\exists n) g_{R_2} \in G_{R_2}(X_2) \exists r_2 \in g_{R_2} \exists r_1' \in g_{R_1}(X_1, r_1[X_1])$$
$$\exists l \in L(l = (r_1', r_2))\}$$

The $(\exists n)x$ denotes that there must be exactly n instances (occurrences) of the variable x satisfying the predicate following it. The semantics of the other variants are similarly defined.

An existential link operator is the case where $\langle q \rangle$ is "≥ 1". If the symbol "+" is specified, $(\exists n)x$ in the above definitions is replaced by $\forall x$. It means that the predicate is satisfied "for all instances of x". The division operation of the relational algebra can be simulated easily by this operator.

We illustrate how this link operator can be applied. Let us use the same schema as in Fig. 2.1 and the same state as in Fig. 2.2. Suppose we want to retrieve all the ENROLLMENTs of the students who took all the core COURSEs offered. An existential link operator is not useful in this case, because it will retrieve all the ENROLLMENTs of the students who took any core COURSEs offered. This query is correctly expressed with a numerical link operator. Figure 2.4 illustrates this example.

Numerical link operators support quantifier ($\langle$c-op$\rangle n$) only at the outer level if there is grouping; within a group, only the existential quantifier may be used. We assume that the former is more common than the latter.

Query 2-2:

Retrieve all the ENROLLMENT occurrences of the students who took all the core courses

Partial DML statement:

COURSE [CORE = "YES"] → // + ENROLLS // (SNO)
→ ENROLLMENT

Result:

{ (20,1,A), (20,2,B), (20,3,C), (30,1,A), (30,2,A) }

Fig. 2.4. Example of numerical link operator

2.3.6.4 Transitive link operators

A transitive link operator (TRN) can be used for a recursive link type. In neutral mode, it retrieves the record occurrences that are connected to at least one occurrence of the initial node by a sequence containing a specified number of link occurrences. In other modes, occurrences of either endpoint are similarly retrieved. It is expressed as:

$$R \to \backslash \langle q \rangle L \backslash \to R$$

where $\langle q \rangle$ is of the form: $\langle c\text{-op} \rangle\, n$. If the $\langle c\text{-op} \rangle$ is omitted, "=" is assumed. The n is either a positive integer number or a symbol "+". The latter denotes the cardinality of R. Setting n to "+" permits the computation of the transitive closure of a link. As mentioned before, we do not allow grouping for this operator. If $\langle q \rangle$ is "$= n$", this operator returns:

Neutral mode:

$$TN_R(n) = \{(r_1, r_n) \;:\; r_1 \in R \wedge r_n \in R \wedge$$
$$\exists l_1 \in L\, \exists\, l_2 \in L \ldots \exists l_{n-1} \in L$$
$$\exists r_2 \in R\, \exists r_3 \in R \ldots \exists\, r_{n-1} \in R$$
$$(l_1 = (r_1, r_2) \wedge l_2 = (r_2, r_3) \wedge \ldots \wedge l_{n-1} = (r_{n-1}, r_n))\}$$

Downward mode:

$$TD_R(n) = \{(r) \;:\; r \in R \wedge \exists l_1 \in L\, \exists l_2 \in L \ldots \exists l_n \in L$$
$$\exists r_1 \in R\, \exists r_2 \in R \ldots \exists r_n \in R$$
$$(l_1 = (r_1, r_2) \wedge l_2 = (r_2, r_3) \wedge \ldots \wedge l_n = (r_n, r))\}$$

Upward mode:

$$TU_R(n) = \{(r) \quad : \quad r \in R \wedge \exists l_1 \in L \, \exists l_2 \in L \ldots \exists l_n \in L$$
$$\exists r_1 \in R \, \exists r_2 \in R \ldots \exists r_n \in R$$
$$(l_1 = (r, r_1) \wedge l_2 = (r_1, r_2) \wedge \ldots \wedge l_n = (r_{n-1}, r_n))\}$$

Other variants can be defined in terms of these definitions. For example, the downward variant where $\langle q \rangle$ is "$\leq n$" is:

$$TD_R(1) \vee TD_R(2) \vee \ldots \vee TD_R(n)$$

Using this link operator, we can, for example, retrieve all the superiors (i.e., managers at every level in a hierarchy) of a given employee. Note that this link operator allows the retrieval of record occurrences that are connected to themselves.

2.3.6.5 Formation of resultant record list type

The last operation of a link operator, a FORM operation, creates a resultant record list type. We use the following notation to describe this operation.

1. $rl|r$ denotes that r is appended to the end of rl.
2. $comp(r, rl, R)$ is a predicate that is true if $r = rl[R]$.

Let *RESULT* be the type of the result of a TRAVERSE operation. Depending on the *MODE*, the FORM returns:

1. Neutral mode:

$$\{rl_1|r_2 \quad : \quad rl_1 \in RL_1 \wedge r_2 \in R_2 \wedge \exists r_1 \in R_1$$
$$(comp(r_1, rl_1, R_1) \wedge (r_1, r_2) \in RESULT)\}$$

2. Downward mode: *RESULT*
3. Upward mode:

$$\{rl_1 \quad : \quad rl_1 \in RL_1 \wedge \exists r_1 \in R_1$$
$$(comp(r_1, rl_1, R_1) \wedge (r_1) \in RESULT)\}$$

2.3.7 Storage Operations

Two storage operations are defined on both records and links. Those operations that violate integrity constraints must be rejected. A record addition operation (RECADD) adds a record occurrence to a record type. If r_1 is added to R_1, then the state of R_1 is:

$$\$R_1 = \$R_1 + \{r_1\}$$

A record deletion operation (RECDEL) deletes a record occurrence from a record type. If r_1 is deleted from R_1, then the state of R_1 becomes:

$$\$R_1 = \$R_1 - \{r_1\}$$

This operation has side effects when the occurrence deleted is incident with some link occurrences. Such link occurrences should be deleted by the system. In our data model, however, no further rippling effect occurs, since each link type is independent of all others.

A link addition (LINKADD) adds a link occurrence l_1 to a link type L_1 as in a record addition operation. The state of L_1 after the operation is:

$$\$L_1 = \$L_1 + \{l_1\}$$

The record occurrences which are incident with this link occurrence must exist for correct execution of this operation.

A link deletion (LINKDEL) deletes one link occurrence l_1 from a link type L_1. The state is changed to:

$$\$L_1 = \$L_1 - \{l_1\}$$

No storage operations are defined for a record list type because it is a transient object defined only at query-processing time.

3. Data Definition Language

3.1 Overview

This chapter describes the Data Definition Language (DDL) of GDL. It is founded on the data model GDM described in the previous chapter. The DDL is used to define the structure, the integrity constraints and views of a schema. It also supports schema evolution. GDL allows the construction of temporary record types and link types that exist only during a single session or run. We say that these objects are *volatile*. Volatile record and link types are described in Chap. 4. The record and link types that reside in the database are said to be *resident*. DDL supports definitions of resident record and link types.

In designing a schema, there are some conflicting factors. For example, records with indices can be accessed faster by using the indices than records without indices; however, each index requires more space, and more time to store and update record occurrences. Because the tradeoffs really depend on applications, it is important to provide a user with some means for *controlling tradeoffs*. This control should be, however, at a logical level. GDL provides two types of access keys to control storage structure of record types. (Keys are described in Sect. 3.2.1.) The inclusion of link types and access keys in a schema definition makes this possible.

GDL makes it possible for a user to design his or her applications using a solely *value-based system*, a solely *link-based system* or any mixture of these systems. A value-based system is a system in which queries are expressed as qualifications on values. A link-based system is one in which queries are expressed as link traversals. A system based on the relational model is a typical value-based system. Conversely, a system based on the CODASYL model is a typical link-based system.

3.2 Schema Definition

A schema definition consists of: a schema name, a list of record type definitions, a list of link type definitions and a list of integrity constraint definitions. The following sections define the functions of the DDL. We use two example schemas in this chapter and the next chapter. Their schema diagrams are illustrated in Figs. 3.1 and 3.2, and their schema definitions are given in Figs. 3.3 and 3.4.

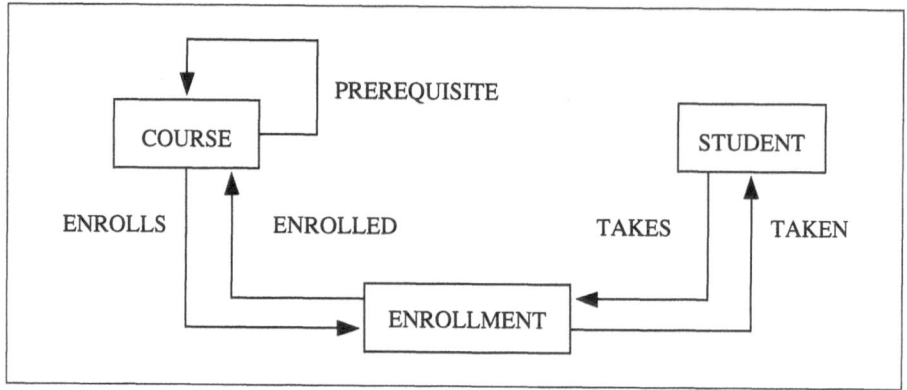

Fig. 3.1. Diagram of educational schema

3.2.1 Record Type Definition

A record type definition is composed of a record type name, a list of attribute definitions and key definitions. The attribute definition consists of an attribute name and a data type definition. The key definitions are optional.

Two types of keys are provided in GDL:

1. *Access keys*: to specify storage structure and access paths of record types.
2. *Unique key*: to specify that the values of a given set of attributes must be unique within a record type.

There are, furthermore, two types of access keys: *clustering key* for physical ordering of record occurrences and *search key* for *indices* on attributes.

Only one clustering key definition is possible for each record type. The clustering key can be a single attribute or a combination of attributes. It specifies that the record occurrences are *clustered* by the values of the clustering key attribute(s). The first key attribute is a major clustering attribute which we call a *primary key attribute*. The values of the second key attribute cluster the record occurrences that have the same value of the first key attribute, and so on. By default, the primary key attribute is defined to be the first attribute appearing in a record type definition. For example, the clustering key attribute of record type COURSE in schema EDUCATIONAL_DATABASE (Fig. 3.1) is CNO by default. A primary key is also provided with an index in our current design of GDL. Sequential access ordered by this attribute is efficient.

Any attribute or any combination of attributes can be defined as a search key. A search key is currently implemented by an index (indices[1]). Any number of search

---

[1]The term "indices" denotes such an "index" that implements a search key consisting of more than one attribute, while "indexes" denotes the plural of "index".

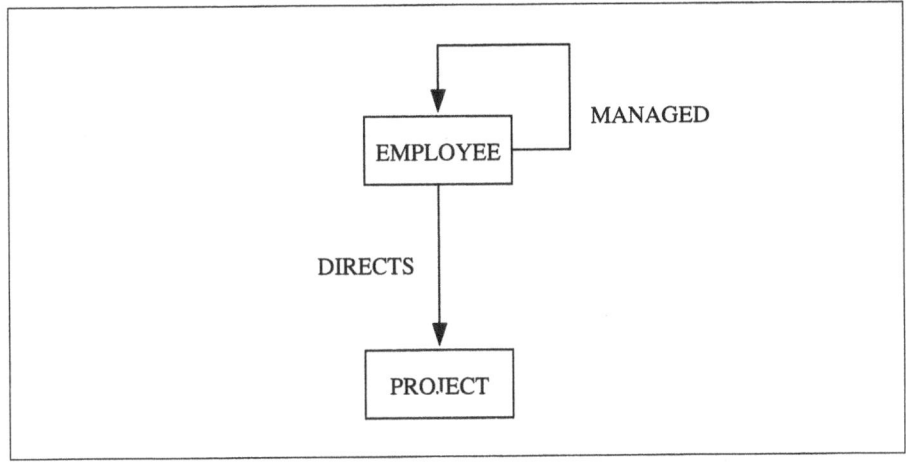

Fig. 3.2. Diagram of enterprise schema

keys can be defined for each record type. A search key declaration tells the system that there may be many queries on this attribute. We create a fast access path for each search key. It is inefficient to search records by an attribute that is neither a primary key nor a search key, unless the number of record occurrences is small. Null values are permitted for search keys.

A unique key can be a single attribute or a combination of attributes. These attributes can also participate in other types of keys at the same time. A unique key declaration specifies that there are no two record occurrences that have the same value of the attribute or the combination of attributes. This is a type of integrity constraint. A unique key is defined only within a record type. Uniqueness constraints spanning more than one record type must be defined in constraint definitions on a schema or views. Null values are not permitted for unique keys.

3.2.2 Link Type Definition

GDL has two classes of link type:

– Real link type
– Virtual link type

For a real link type, which is the default, the occurrences always physically exist. It can be an *essential link type* that bears information, or a *non-essential link type* that bears no information. In the latter case, an attribute of the terminal node record type must be compatible with at least one of the attributes of the initial node record type.

In case of non-essential link types, it is possible to link two record types without physically storing link occurrences. For example, consider the link TAKES from STUDENT to ENROLLMENT, in schema EDUCATIONAL_DATABASE

---

define schema EDUCATIONAL-DATABASE

record COURSE
| | attribute | CNO | integer | |
| | attribute | CNAME | character | 10 |

record COURSE
attribute	CNO	integer	
attribute	CNAME	character	10
attribute	DEPT	character	10
attribute	CORE	character	3
search key	CNAME		
unique key	CNO		

record ENROLLMENT
attribute	SNO	integer	
attribute	CNO	integer	
attribute	GRADE	character	2

record STUDENT
attribute	SNO	integer	
attribute	SNAME	character	30
attribute	MAJOR	character	10
search key	SNAME		
unique key	SNO		

link PREREQUISITE   (COURSE, COURSE)

link ENROLLS, ENROLLED   (COURSE, ENROLLMENT)

link TAKES   (STUDENT, ENROLLMENT)
    virtual   SNO = SNO

link TAKEN   (ENROLLMENT, STUDENT)
    virtual   SNO = SNO

Fig. 3.3. Definition of educational schema

(Figs. 3.1, 3.3). We can retrieve efficiently all the enrollments of a given student identified by SNO, by searching identical values of SNO in ENROLLMENT since this SNO is the primary key of ENROLLMENT. That is, if the terminal node record type of a link type has a fast access path on a particular attribute and the initial node record type contains the compatible attribute, the DBMS can efficiently implement link traversals without physically storing link occurrences. The access path on the terminal node record type *virtually links* two record types. We define the semantics of a virtual link type from record type R_1 (having an attribute A_1) to record type R_2 (having an attribute A_2) as follows:

$$\{(r_1, r_2) \quad : \quad r_1 \in R_1 \wedge r_2 \in R_2 \wedge r_1[A_1] \langle \text{c-op} \rangle r_2[A_2]\}$$

where A_1 and A_2 are compatible and A_2 is either a primary key or a search key. The $\langle \text{c-op} \rangle$ is one of the comparison operators defined in Chap. 2. This is similar to a join defined by E. F. Codd [20]. Arbitrary join predicates can be defined on virtual link types in view definitions.

Virtual link types are used in DML statements just like real link types except that no storage operations are possible on these link types. Note that if we use only

```
        define schema ENTERPRISE
        record EMPLOYEE
                attribute          ENO             integer         10
                attribute          NAME            character       30
                attribute          SALARY          integer
                clustering key     NAME
                search key         ENO
                unique key         ENO

        record PROJECT
                attribute          PNO             integer
                attribute          NAME            character       20
                attribute          MANAGER         integer         10
                clustering key     NAME
                search key         PNO
                unique key         PNO

        link DIRECTS                       (EMPLOYEE, PROJECT)

        link MANAGED                       (EMPLOYEE, EMPLOYEE)

        constraint link DIRECTS (EMPLOYEE, PROJECT) always
            path EMPLOYEE → /DIRECTS/ → PROJECT :
        EMPLOYEE.ENO = PROJECT. MANAGER

        constraint link MANAGED (E1, E2) never
            path E1 → /MANAGED/ → E2 : E1. SALARY ≧ E2. SALARY
```

Fig. 3.4. Definition of enterprise schema

virtual link types to connect record types, GDL becomes a value-based system. One demerit is that all the link types used in queries must be defined prior to their use.

The name of an inverse link type may be specified in the definition of a link type. Otherwise, it is referenced by the name of the corresponding link type prefixed with a %.

3.2.3 Constraint Definition

We take an *operational approach* to supporting integrity constraints, views and schema evolution as in many relational systems. GDL provides the user with an assertion language that allows him or her to specify integrity constraints, views and schema evolution using the same language constructs as in the DML. This approach simplifies DBMS architecture and preserves a uniform system to the user. Furthermore, all the expressive power of the DML is available to these facilities without expanding the DBMS. The DML will be discussed in the next chapter.

An integrity constraint defines a restriction on permissible states of a schema. The numerical link operator (NUM) is useful for representing *functional dependencies*. Due to the power of link operators, integrity constraints of GDL can express not only first-order predicates but also higher-order predicates.

An integrity constraint is checked only when a storage operation on the object in question is invoked, because only storage operations change the schema state. GDL provides two modes of integrity constraints: "never" and "always". In the *negative mode* specified by "never", the DBMS tries to select record or link occurrences using an expression supplied by the user. If no occurrences are retrieved, the constraints are *satisfied*. Otherwise, the storage operation must be rejected. In the *affirmative mode* specified by "always", the operation in question is satisfied if one or more occurrences are retrieved. Although one of these modes is theoretically enough to express integrity constraints, we decided to have two modes to improve efficiency.

Two examples of a constraint definition are given in Fig. 3.4. The first one specifies that if an occurrence of EMPLOYEE is connected to an occurrence of PROJECT via link type DIRECTS, then the value of ENO in EMPLOYEE must be the same as the value of MANAGER in PROJECT. The second example specifies that the salary of any manager is lower than none of his or her subordinates' salaries. Note that a constraint definition is never specified for a virtual link type, since storage operations are not defined on this link type.

3.3 Views

The definition of views permits more than one application to share a database securely and conveniently. A view definition is composed of a view name together with a list of record and link type definitions. The record and link definitions specify not only record and link structure but also mappings that describe how these are derived from a schema. These mappings are specified in terms of a record selection expression or a link selection expression against an underlying schema. Each query against a given view will be modified to be consistent with the view definition. The occurrences of a view are not copied into separate storage in our current design. This approach saves storage and avoids the problems of inconsistency between the state of a view and the state of its underlying schema, although it can be inefficient if the view is used frequently.

We give an example of a view, PUBLIC_CS_DATABASE, on schema EDUCATIONAL_DATABASE. This view allows the user to see public documents in the Department of Computer Sciences ("CS"). Figures 3.5 and 3.6 show the diagram of this view and the view definition, respectively. It consists of two record types, COURSE and STUDENT, and two link types, PREREQUISITE and TAKEN. COURSE represents the courses offered in the Department of Computer Sciences. STUDENT represents the students whose major is Computer Sciences. Note that if some courses in the Department of Computer Sciences have prerequisite courses that are not within the department, the latter are not included in PREREQUISITE. A similar discussion also holds for TAKEN.

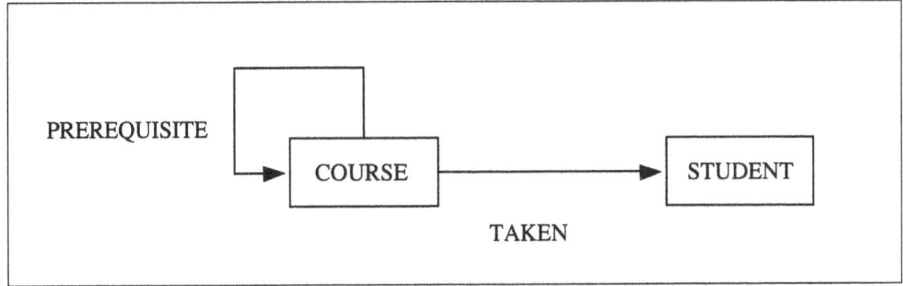

Fig. 3.5. Diagram of PUBLIC_CS_DATABASE view

define view PUBLIC_CS_DATABASE
  on schema EDUCATIONAL_DATABASE

record COURSE (CNO, CNAME, CORE)
  from COURSE [DEPT = "CS"] (CNO, CNAME, CORE)

record STUDENT (SNAME)
  from STUDENT [MAJOR = "CS"] (SNAME)

link PREREQUISITE (COURSE, COURSE)
  from PREREQUISITE [path COURSE [DEPT = "CS"]
    → /PREREQUISITE/ → COURSE [DEPT = "CS"]]

link TAKEN (COURSE, STUDENT)
  from (COURSE, STUDENT) [path COURSE [DEPT = "CS"]
    → /ENROLLS/ → ENROLLMENT → /TAKEN/ →
    STUDENT [MAJOR = "CS"]]

Fig. 3.6. Definition of PUBLIC_CS_DATABASE view

3.4 Schema Evolution

A user may occasionally need to change the definition of his or her schema.
Changes in a schema definition may propagate to the databases and/or application
programs. To complete schema evolution, we must also handle these side effects.
Table 3.1 gives the relationships between types of change and their effects on
environments. By an effect on a database, we mean that some *existent* database(s)
must be *converted* whether the effect is a side effect or not. Similarly, by an effect on
an application program, we mean that those existent application programs that
refer to the schema need to be converted.

Schema evolution can be processed in two ways:

1. Using only the DDL: A user specifies both a definition of an evolved schema,
   and how to derive the new schema from an existent database.

Table 3.1. Types of schema change and their effects

Object	Add	Delete	Replace
Data type of attribute	—	—	A, D
Clustering key	—	—	A, D
Search key	N	A	—
Unique key	D	A	A, D
Attribute	A, D	A, D	—
Record type	N	A	—
Real/virtual	—	—	D
Endpoint record type	—	—	A, D
Link type	N	A	—
Constraint	D	A	A, D

where A denotes effect on existent applications
      D denotes effect on existent databases
      N denotes no effect on both
      — denotes "not applicable"

2. Using both DDL and DML: A user creates a new definition of a schema by the DDL; then uses select statements in the DML, to retrieve the occurrences in temporary areas, called volatile types (described in Sect. 4.2); and finally uses add statements, to store the occurrences into new types that have been defined by the DDL.

As we see in Table 3.1, the addition of a search key, a record type and a link type has no effect on existent databases and application programs in our architecture. In many cases, the conversion of an application program can be avoided by defining a view on the new schema, although this may cause poor performance. Schema changes that cause conversions of databases and/or application programs should be minimized because these conversions are costly. Schema evolution will generally be accomplished by deriving new record types and link types from existent databases one by one.

4. Data Manipulation Language

4.1 Overview

This chapter describes the Data Manipulation Language (DML). The Elementary Data Language discussed in Chap. 2 provides a useful repertoire of operations on network structure. Like an assembly language, however, it is tedious to write queries in the Elementary Data Language. To provide a user with a higher-level language facility, we have designed a DML on top of the Elementary Data Language. The DML defines rules for composition of Elementary Data Operations. The design goals of DML are summarized as:

- Easy to write queries.
- Aid the user to construct efficient queries.
- Precise definition of each DML statement.

To achieve these goals, we take the following approach:

- Queries are formulated in terms of traversals of the schema.
- Set-at-a-time representation of DML.
- Close correspondence between each DML statement and its actual processing.
- Each DML statement is uniquely translated into a sequence of Elementary Data Operations.
- The user can manipulate not only record types but also link types.
- Dynamic creation and deletion of record types and link types are allowed.

GDL supports a very *versatile* DBMS architecture. DML provides a user with powerful tools for sophisticated database operations. These language features allow an advanced user to *efficiently tailor* databases for his or her applications. At the same time, a beginner can write a query with very little knowledge of GDL. For example, such a user does not need to know link manipulations. To retrieve record occurrences of a schema, he or she only needs to know expressions for selecting records.

The following sections describe prominent features of DML. A full and precise definition of the syntax is given in Appendix A. It should be noted that all the record types and link types must be defined before being referenced.

4.2 Volatile Object Definition

The DML supports volatile record and link types. Volatile types differ from resident types in several aspects. They can be defined only in a DML program or an interactive query session. They are stored in simple arrays that are created in a user's area by a DML processor or a query processor. The user and the system can both access the arrays. The naming convention depends on the host language. Volatile record and link types can be used as an area for data passing between an application program and the system. No key definitions are allowed for volatile record types.

As we will describe in the next section, the record and link occurrences retrieved are stored in volatile record and link types specified by the user. To support schema evolution, these occurrences can be inserted into a new schema by "add record" and "add link" statements. The new schema must be defined prior to loading data.

4.3 Record Selection and Creation

4.3.1 Variables

A variable represents a set of qualified occurrences of a given type. Record type names and link type names themselves are used to denote variables in DML statements. When a single record type is referenced more than once in a single DML statement, however, ambiguity may occur. A record type name can be associated with more than one different qualified set. For example, record type EMPLOYEE can be associated with both subordinates and managers. To distinguish different qualified sets, we provide *variable statements*. One example of a variable statement is:

VARIABLE EMPLOYEE: E1, E2

4.3.2 Record Selection

Selection of record occurrences is expressed by a *selection expression* which is one of the basic language constructs of the DML. It is used not only for record selection but also for link selection since a link occurrence is identified by a pair of record occurrences. A qualification for record or link selection may involve only one record type or relationships between record types. This section describes the former case and the following sections describe the latter case.

A qualification that involves a single record type is called an intra-record restriction (IRST). Consider the enterprise schema (Fig. 3.2). An example of an IRST on record type EMPLOYEE is:

NAME = "SMITH"

In a general form, a qualification may have more than one restriction connected by set operators $(+, -, \cap)$. For example,

$$\text{NAME} = \text{``SMITH''} \cap \text{SALARY} > 30000$$

Parentheses may be used to change a regular left-to-right evaluation order.

4.3.3 Path Expressions

In a query that involves more than one record type, the record types referenced in the query must have some relationship to the record type(s) to be retrieved which we call *target record type*(s). (A user specifies the target record type(s).) This means that the desired record types are in some way *connected* to the target record type(s) in the GDL graph when all the relationships between record types are expressed by link types. Whether link types are volatile or resident does not make a difference at the representation level of a query.

To express the structure of connected record types, we extend the concept of *path* [40]. The usual definition of a path is a finite alternating sequence of record types and link types beginning and ending with record types, such that for each link type, the preceding record type is the initial node record type of the link type and the following record type is the terminal node record type of the link type. We expand this notion of a path by *including operations* on record types and link types on a path. We call this structure a *path expression*. That is, a path expression is an expression of a sequence of record restrictions and link traversals.

> $\langle$path expression$\rangle :: =$
>> $\langle$path expression$\rangle \rightarrow \langle$link operator$\rangle \rightarrow \langle$record clause$\rangle |$
>> $\langle$record clause$\rangle \rightarrow \langle$link operator$\rangle \rightarrow \langle$record clause$\rangle$
>
> $\langle$record clause$\rangle :: =$
>> $\langle$record name$\rangle |$
>> $\langle$record name$\rangle [\langle$selection expression$\rangle] |$
>> $(\langle$record name$\rangle [\langle$selection expression$\rangle])$

When a record clause for a terminal node is enclosed by parentheses, the terminal node will be evaluated before the traversal operation.

Let us give an example of a path. Suppose we have a query that selects those employees who directly manage employee "SMITH" for the enterprise schema illustrated in Fig. 3.2. We reference two types of EMPLOYEE, declaring E1 and E2 as the variables of EMPLOYEE. E1 denotes the employee called "SMITH" and E2 denotes the managers of E1. We can express this qualification easily by a single path expression.

$$\text{path E1}[\text{NAME} = \text{``SMITH''}] \rightarrow /\text{MANAGED}/ \rightarrow \text{E2}$$

An intra-record restriction (i.e., NAME = "SMITH") is specified for E1 to find employee(s) called "SMITH". Symbols enclosing link type names indicate the types of link operators to be operated on the link types: / / for an existential link operator, // // for a numerical link operator, and \ \ for a transitive link operator.

If the query is modified to select all the superiors of EMPLOYEE "SMITH", then the path expression will have a *transitive link operator* instead of an existential link operator:

$$\text{path E1[NAME} = \text{"SMITH"}] \rightarrow \backslash + \text{MANAGED} \backslash \rightarrow \text{E2}$$

Every path must follow the direction of the link types appearing on the path. (Of course, inverse link types can be used to follow the path.)

The *positions of target record types* on a given path determine the *mode* of each link operator. On the left of the leftmost target record type, the terminal node record type of each link type is always the target of the link operator (i.e., a downward mode). Those link operators in between the leftmost and rightmost target record types have a neutral mode. The link operators on the right of the rightmost target record type also have a neutral mode, except the last link operator, which has an upward mode. The modes of link operators appearing on inner nested paths are recursively defined. The constraint that record types appearing in a query must be connected via some path does not reduce the power of the language, since the user can create link types on the fly if necessary.

4.3.4 Inter-Record Restrictions

A path can be followed by a qualification that specifies restriction(s) spanning more than one record type on the path. Such a restriction is called an *inter-record restriction* (XRST) as opposed to an intra-record restriction. The predicate that the salary of a manager is lower than that of his/her subordinates can be expressed as:

$$\text{path E1} \rightarrow \text{/MANAGED/} \rightarrow \text{E2: E1.SALARY} > \text{E2.SALARY}$$

As in an intra-record restriction, restrictions in an inter-record restriction can be connected by set operators and parenthesized.

4.3.5 Nested Path Expressions

Nested paths are allowed in the DML. This is useful to express the situation where a record type on a path must be further qualified by another path expression or where other target record types are on another path(s). Consider the enterprise schema. The predicate the employees named "SMITH", E1, direct PROJECT and are managed by employee E2 can be expressed by a nested path expression:

$$\text{path E1[path E1[NAME} = \text{"SMITH"}] \rightarrow \text{/DIRECTS/}$$
$$\rightarrow \text{PROJECT]} \rightarrow \text{/MANAGED/} \rightarrow \text{E2}$$

4.3.6 Set Operators

Path expressions can be connected by set operators $(+, -, \cap)$. If two path expressions are connected by a set operator, both path expressions must contain the same target record type. Otherwise, the set operation is undefined. An example is a query that selects employees who manage employee "SMITH" or who direct project "DBMS":

$$(\text{path } E1[NAME = \text{"SMITH"}] \rightarrow /MANAGED/ \rightarrow E2)$$
$$+ (\text{path } E2 \rightarrow /DIRECTS/ \rightarrow PROJECT[NAME = \text{"DBMS"}])$$

E2 must be specified as the target record type in the DML statement.

4.3.7 Select Record Statement

The select record statement is used to select record occurrences of one or more record types and to construct occurrences of a new record type from them. The syntax for the select record statement is:

select record ⟨record name⟩: = ⟨target record list⟩
{[⟨selection expression⟩]} {⟨projection⟩} {⟨sorting⟩}

Items enclosed by curly brackets are optional. The record name in this statement specifies the *destination record type* into which the retrieved record occurrences are to be brought. We restrict a destination record type to being volatile. Both the user and the system can access the destination record type, and no special communication area is necessary. The record list in the statement specifies target record type(s), while the selection expression specifies qualification of the target record type(s). If no selection expression is specified, all the occurrences of the target record type(s) are retrieved.

The projection part gives a specification of a projection operation including null and default value assignments. If this part is absent, the whole record is copied to the destination record type. The sorting part gives a specification for sorting on the destination record type.

An example of a select record statement is shown in Fig. 4.1. The parenthesized NAME in the second GDL statement specifies a projection on E2 to retrieve only one attribute NAME. MANAGERS is the destination record type of this record selection statement.

The next example contains an inter-record restriction. If the constraint on a manager's salary defined in Fig. 3.4 is not enforced, there might be managers who are paid less than their subordinates. The DML statement in Fig. 4.2 retrieves such managers. The restriction on SALARY is between two record types, E1 and E2, connected by link MANAGED.

Figure 4.3 shows an example of a more complex query for the educational database shown in Fig. 3.1. Its intent is to retrieve those students who took COURSE "386" but who have not actually taken its prerequisite courses. The DML statement can be decomposed into three path expressions. Note that this is not the only way to express the query in GDL. We can, for example, decompose the GDL statement into two statements to avoid redundant evaluation of the intra-record restriction on COURSE.

The final example shows how we create a new record type that consists of attributes of more than one existent record type. Suppose we need to create a record type that is composed of an employee's name, and his or her manager's name. Figure 4.4 gives a DML statement for this query.

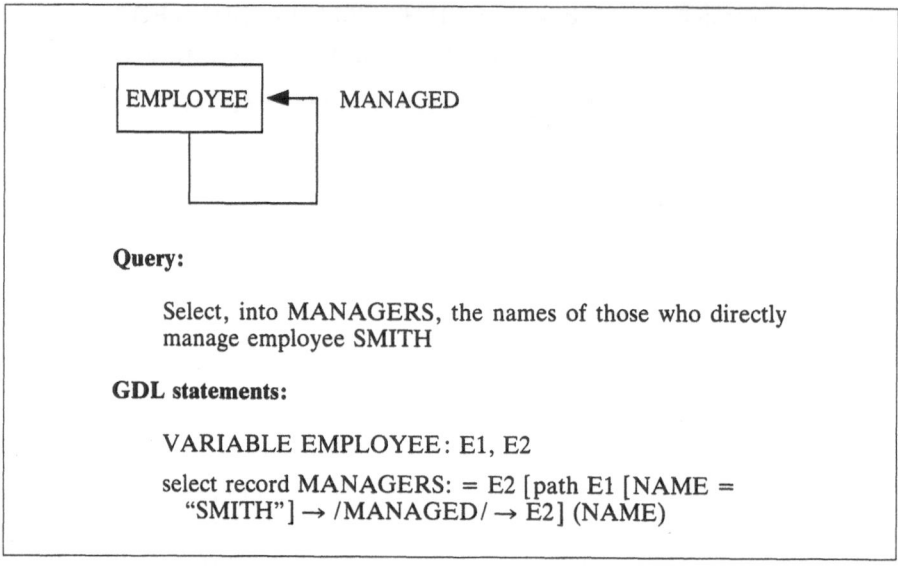

Query:

   Select, into MANAGERS, the names of those who directly
   manage employee SMITH

GDL statements:

   VARIABLE EMPLOYEE: E1, E2

   select record MANAGERS: = E2 [path E1 [NAME =
      "SMITH"] → /MANAGED/ → E2] (NAME)

Fig. 4.1. Example of simple record selection statement

Query:

   Select the managers (LOW-PAY-MANAGER) whose salaries
   are lower than at least one of their direct subordinates

GDL statements:

   VARIABLE EMPLOYEE: E1, E2

   select record LOW-PAY-MANAGER: = E2 [path E1 →
      /MANAGED/ → E2: E1. SALAY > E2. SALARY]

Fig. 4.2. Example of inter-record restriction

These examples show how easily queries are expressed in GDL. As we see, writing a query merely involves tracing path(s) in a graph representing a given schema.

4.3.8 Translation of DML Statements

Each DML statement is translated into a sequence of Elementary Data Operations. The evaluation of a given selection expression is executed from left to right unless parentheses or nested path expressions are encountered. In this case, the

---

Query:

> Select the students, into SKIP-STUDENT, who took "386"
> but who actually have not taken its prerequisite courses

GDL statements:

VARIABLE COURSE: C1, C2, C3

select record SKIP-STUDENT: = STUDENT [path
    ENROLLMENT [path C1 [CNO = 386] → /ENROLLS/
    (SNO) → ENROLLMENT → (SNO)// ⊧ + ENROLLED //
    → (C3 [path C2 [CNO = 386] → /PREREQUISITE/ →
    C3])] → /TAKEN/ → STUDENT]

Fig. 4.3. Example of complex query

Query:

> Get all pairs of an employee and his/her direct manager

GDL statements:

VARIABLE EMPLOYEE: E1, E2

select record EMP-MNG: = E1, E2
    [path E1 → /MANAGED/ → E2]
    (ENAME: = E1.NAME, MNAME: = E2.NAME)

Fig. 4.4. Example of new record type creation

inner expressions are evaluated before the outer expression, as in usual mathematical expressions. A path expression is evaluated along the direction of the path. The record clause for a given terminal node record type can be parenthesized; in this case, the record clause will be evaluated before the link traversal. The select-record statement in Fig. 4.1 is translated into:

1. Restriction on E1 (RST)
   $\langle E1' \rangle := \langle E1 \rangle$ [E1.NAME = "SMITH"]
2. Existential link operator on MANAGED (EXT)
   E2: = $\langle E1' \rangle$ [downward mode: E1' → /MANAGED/ → E2] $\langle E2 \rangle$
3. Projection on E2' (PROJ)
   MANAGERS: = $\langle E2' \rangle$ (E2'.NAME)

The items enclosed by angular brackets denote record list types. Chapter 5 describes the translation of DML statements.

4.3.9 Graph-Driven Interactive Query Interface

The design of an interactive query interface is beyond the scope of this work. The DML is, however, closely tied with our strategy for the interactive query interface. Therefore, we give a brief summary of the system being designed. Our interactive query interface is *graph-driven*, supported by graphics packages. It can be summarized as follows:

1. The user selects a schema.
2. The system shows a diagram (a graph) of the schema on a CRT screen.
3. The user points to record types (nodes) and link types (arcs) alternately to draw a path representing his/her query.
4. At each node to which a user points, the system asks the user for its qualification expression.
5. At each arc of the path, the system asks the user which link operator should be applied.

This system can be implemented by a rather simple graphics system and a query processor. It is easy for the user to formulate queries using such an interface, because the approach is very visual and natural. Its power becomes even more evident if a query involves many record types and link types. GDL is obviously a suitable data language for the graph-driven query system since the mapping between the user language and GDL is one to one.

4.4 Link Selection and Creation

GDL allows the user to manipulate explicitly links as well as records. An occurrence of a given link type can be identified by an occurrence of a binary record list type that consists of the two node record types associated with the link type. Selection and creation of link occurrences can be done via the manipulation of occurrences of the corresponding binary record list type. The select link statement is used to select or to create a link type composed of two *connected* record types, while the create link statement is used to create a link type composed of two *unconnected* record types. Note that the select link and the connect link statements permit the user to establish new relationships between two record types.

4.4.1 Select Link Statement

The select link statement is used to select occurrences of a given link type or to create a link type that is defined between two connected record types. Its syntax is:

$$\text{select link} \langle \text{link name} \rangle := \langle \text{link clause} \rangle$$

where

$$\langle \text{link clause} \rangle ::= \langle \text{link name} \rangle \{ (\langle \text{record name} \rangle ,$$
$$\langle \text{record name} \rangle) \} \{ [\langle \text{selection expression} \rangle] \}$$

The first link name in this statement specifies a *destination link type* into which qualified occurrences are brought. The link clause specifies a target link type, its endpoints and its qualification. The *target link type* is a link type whose occurrences are to be retrieved. Its qualification is expressed by a selection expression, as in the select record statement, where target record types are the initial and terminal node record types of the target link type.

For example, we can select link occurrences of a link type called LOW‒PAY‒MANAGED from link type MANAGED in schema ENTERPRISE by:

$$\text{select link LOW‒PAY‒MANAGED} := \text{MANAGED (E1, E2)}$$
$$[\text{path E1} \rightarrow /\text{MANAGED}/ \rightarrow \text{E2}:$$
$$\text{E1.SALARY} > \text{E2.SALARY}]$$

This is a link version of query 3 shown in Fig. 4.2.

4.4.2 Connect Link Statement

This statement enables a user to create a new link type between two unconnected record types. Its syntax is:

$$\text{connect link } \langle \text{link name} \rangle := $$
$$(\langle \text{record clause} \rangle, \langle \text{record clause} \rangle)$$
$$[\langle \text{link creation condition} \rangle]$$

The initial and terminal node record types can be independently qualified. The link creation condition is either a Cartesian product, denoted by "*", or an inter-record expression. The link creation condition is translated into a link creation operation.

Suppose we originally did not have the link type DIRECTS in schema ENTERPRISE. We can easily create this by a connect link statement, as shown in Fig. 4.5. That is, we construct link type DIRECTS that links the occurrence of record type EMPLOYEE to that of record type PROJECT if the value of ENO of EMPLOYEE is the same as that of MANAGER of PROJECT.

Intent:

Construct a link type called DIRECTS which connects
EMPLOYEE to PROJECT if the employee is the manager of
the project

GDL statement:

connect link DIRECTS: = (EMPLOYEE, PROJECT)
    [EMPLOYEE.ENO = PROJECT. MANAGER]

Fig. 4.5. Example of connect link statement

4.5 Storage Operations

Storage operations on both record and link types are described in this section. They are translated into corresponding storage operations of the Elementary Data Operations. All the target record and link types described in the remainder of this chapter must be volatile. Destination record and link types can be either resident or volatile.

4.5.1 Add Record Statement

To copy the occurrences of a record type into another record type, we have an add record statement. The syntax of the add record statement is:

> add record ⟨target record type⟩ to ⟨destination record type⟩

Record occurrences of the target record type are copied to the destination record type. It can be input by the user or derived from the current database by using a select record statement. The target record type and the destination record type should have the same composition of compatible attributes. We say that two such record types are *compatible*. Note that this statement does not change the state of the target record type.

4.5.2 Add Link Statement

This statement allows the user to copy the occurrences of a link type to another link type. The syntax is:

> add link ⟨target link type⟩ to ⟨destination link type⟩

As in the add record statement, this operation can be used to input link occurrences. Let us define compatible link types: if two link types have both a compatible initial node record type and a compatible terminal node record type, then they are called *compatible link types*. The target link type should be compatible with the destination link type. The add link statement is successfully executed only if initial and terminal node record occurrences actually exist. It does not change the state of the target link type.

4.5.3 Delete Record (Link) Statement

A delete record/delete link statement allows a user to delete the record/link occurrences of the target record/link type from the source record/link type. This is a set difference operation. The syntax is:

> delete record ⟨target record type⟩ from ⟨source record type⟩
>
> delete link ⟨target link type⟩ from ⟨source link type⟩

The target type and the source type should be compatible. This operation does not change the state of the target record/link type. If the record occurrence deleted is an initial or terminal node record occurrence of any link occurrence, then those link occurrences are also deleted.

Intent:

Update link DIRECTS such that REAGAN (ENO = 2)
directs PROJUSA instead of CARTER (ENO = 1)

GDL statement:

reconnect link DIRECTS
[path EMPLOYEE [ENO = 1] → /DIRECTS/ →
PROJECT [NAME = "PROJUSA"]] initial node: =
EMPLOYEE [ENO = 2]

Fig. 4.6. Example of reconnect link statement

4.5.4 Remove Record (Link) Statement

These statements provide another form of deletion for a record/link type. They delete the record/link occurrences that satisfy a given qualification. The qualification is specified in the same way as in the select record/link statement. Its syntax is:

remove record ⟨record clause⟩

remove link ⟨link clause⟩

As in the delete record statement, the execution of the remove record statement may invalidate the existence of the link occurrences whose initial or terminal node record occurrences are removed by the statement.

4.5.5 Replace Record Statement

We can replace values of some attributes of a record type by a replace record statement. Record occurrences to be replaced are specified by the record clause previously described. The syntax of the replace record statement is:

replace record ⟨record clause⟩ (⟨replace attribute list⟩)

The replace attribute list is a list of replacement specifications, each of which consists of an attribute to be replaced and a new value.

4.5.6 Reconnect Link Statement

We can update link occurrences by this statement. Its syntax is:

reconnect link ⟨link clause⟩ ⟨reconnect node⟩

The link clause specifies the link occurrences to be changed. The reconnect node specifies which node record type is to be changed and the new node record occurrence(s). The latter is specified by a record clause. Figure 4.6 shows an example of a reconnect link statement.

5. Implementation of GDL

5.1 Overview

This chapter defines and describes an implementation design for GDL. The GDL concept of defining *logical access paths* as an intrinsic part of data definition yields a system with a high degree of integration between the DDL processor/DML precompiler and the run-time system. The data definition tables established by the DDL processor are used by the DML precompiler not only to generate appropriate code for data manipulation but also to effect local optimization of expressions within DML statements.

DML statements consist of sequences of operations from the GDM described in Chap. 2. This mapping is accomplished basically by a simple left-to-right scan (as shown later in the chapter; see Fig. 5.9). The run-time system can and does directly implement the Elementary Data Operations. Elementary Data Operations are mapped by the precompiler directly to physical storage operations.

These latter two factors combine to give a very simple structure to the run-time system and a very short call depth to execute a query. The run-time system consists essentially of only the levels illustrated in Fig. 5.1. The short call depth to process a query is one of the major contributing factors to efficient CPU processing.

The implementation design given in this chapter follows the flow of data through the creation of data definitions by the DDL processor, through their use by the DML precompiler and query processor, to execution of Elementary Data Operations against these data structures, and finally to physical storage operations.

GDL is characterized by its graphical representation of data relationships and its explicit manipulation of links. Therefore, we put emphasis on implementation support for these features in our descriptions of all the components of the system. Implementation of integrity control and view support are briefly described. We do not, however, discuss implementation of other facilities of a full database management system, such as a report generator or a recovery facility. Concurrency control can be handled as cleanly as in the relational model, because each record type and each link type are treated as individual objects in our system.

The design goals for the implementation are:

– Structured design
– High performance

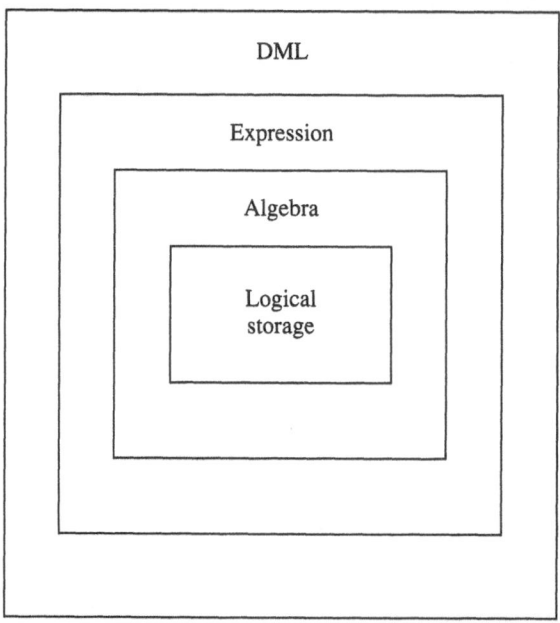

Fig. 5.1. Representation levels in a GDL-based system

– Simplicity
– Independence from specific operating environments

To obtain high performance for query evaluation, we specifically targeted the following goals:

– Minimize the number of I/O operations
– Minimize the number of record fetches to keep necessary records in core
– Maximize locality in working space
– Cluster records by clustering key

Our proposed system configuration is given in Fig. 5.2. Major components of a DBMS include:

1. DDL processor
2. DML precompiler
3. Run-time system
4. Query processor

The arrows represent information flows in the system, and the double line arrows represent information directly supplied by users.

A schema definition must be processed by the DDL processor prior to the use of DML statements for the schema. The processing of DML statements embedded in a host language has two phases:

1. Translating DML statements into target host-language statements
2. Executing the translated statements with the run-time system

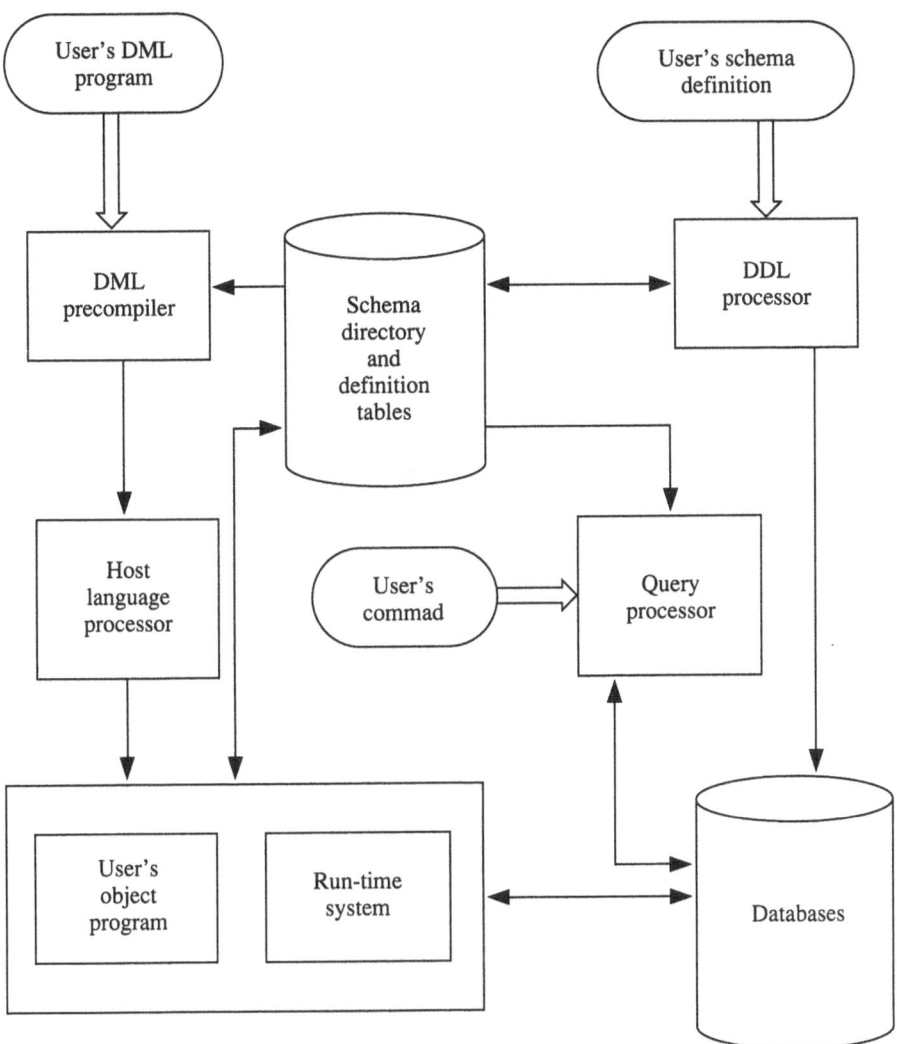

Fig. 5.2. System configuration

5.2 Some Design Issues

This section describes some major issues relating to our approach in the design of a GDL-based system: particularly, evaluation of path expressions, implementation of record lists, storage structures for link occurrences, and concurrency control.

Query processing in GDL is rather straightforward because a query expressed by a path expression is close to the decomposed form described by Wong and Youssefi [76]. They later [81] showed that "reduction" is almost always a good tactic in the decomposition of a query. Formulating a query by a path expression in GDL is actually performing a reduction at query definition time. To keep our system compact, we do not support global optimization. Without it, the query evaluation in GDL yields reasonable efficiency because the system enforces the existence of access paths on relationships between record types in a query.

This system can, however, easily incorporate optimization of intra-record restrictions and of expressions that contain only one link operator, i.e., the simplest form of path expressions. In the relational model, the latter is called a two-variable query. Chapter 6 describes possible alternatives for query evaluation for two-variable queries.

We represent the record list described in Chap. 2 as a URI-tuple. A URI-tuple is a tuple of unique record identifiers (abbreviated URIs). Most Elementary Data Operations can be formulated as manipulation of URI-tuples. One of the advantages of this strategy is that the length of each element of a URI-tuple is fixed (probably one word). The type of a URI-tuple has one-to-one correspondence with the record list type that it represents.

In an actual implementation, URIs can be implemented directly as logical record addresses, or simply as unique identifiers. In the latter case, the system must support a directory to the logical record addresses. This indirection eases the maintenance of referential integrity when record occurrences are deleted or moved. It requires, however, an extra access to the directory before accessing a record occurrence. Which approach to choose depends on the characteristics of applications. For a rather static application where record update is infrequent, the first approach is appropriate. The second approach may be taken for dynamic applications. In our current design (see Appendix B), we chose the first alternative.

Link occurrences are stored separately from record occurrences. Our storage structure for link occurrences is similar to that for indices. It consists of a tree-structured file and a flat file. The tree-structured file is organized by the values of URIs of an initial node. The flat file contains actual link occurrences, sorted by the values of the URIs of the initial node. Access to record occurrences through the separately stored link occurrences is slower than one through embedded link occurrences because of an extra access to the link storage. The following are, however, the advantages of our approach over the embedded link approach:

- It is easy to support schema evolution, because additions and deletions of link types can be done without changing the storage structure for the endpoint record types.
- Simpler storage structure for record types.
- Reduction in the record file size which allows a faster scan on record storage.
- Reduction in the number of record accesses for some semi-joins.

An intra-record restriction on a record type can be evaluated only by indices. If this record type is not a target record type and not used in an inter-record restriction, further access to the record occurrences is not needed.

As we have mentioned in Chap. 2, upon the creation of a link type, its inverse link type is automatically created by the system. When a terminal node occurrence of a link type is deleted, its inverse link type is used to identify the corresponding initial node.

For concurrency control and recovery, GDL can be easily expanded to include the definition of transactions. A transaction defines a unit of work where the integrity of a database is maintained before and after the transaction. The degree of consistency of a database [36] can be controlled by a user in terms of this transaction definition. A transaction may span many DML statements or a DML statement containing a path expression. Within a single path expression, there are also possibilities of different degrees of consistency. Whether all the record and link types (or their occurrences) in a given path should be locked until the end of evaluation of the expression, or not, depends on the degree of consistency that a user requires. If all the record and link types (occurrences) in a path expression are not locked, the system must properly handle the incidences of deleted record and link occurrences during the processing of the expression.

The degree of concurrency of the system [36] is determined by the underlying lock mechanism that controls concurrent transactions; the granularity of locks and the protocol for locks determine this. There are at least four levels of granularity: schemas, views, record and link types, and occurrences.

A GDL user can define a transaction as easily as in the relational system. The set-at-a-time query representation allows concise expression of a processing task. In GDL, the physical placement of records is independent of that of links. A user writes DML statements without any consideration on physical structures, unlike the statements in a CODASYL network model or in a hierarchical model. A path expression is a specification of logical relationships among records, even though it can be easily mapped onto physical access paths.

GDL does not allow a deletion operation to propagate automatically beyond incident links or endpoint records. If the propagation of a deletion of a given node to the sub-tree rooted from it is desired, as seen in a hierarchical data model, it should be explicitly expressed by a constraint definition. When a system provides access paths such as indices and links, referential integrity becomes a problem. Especially, in an environment where concurrent access to a database is allowed, the system must securely maintain the referential integrity within a reasonable time constraint. If either or both endpoint occurrences of a link occurrence are deleted, the link occurrence must also be deleted. Indices must be updated whenever the values of records for the corresponding attributes change.

5.3 DDL Processor

5.3.1 Functions of DDL Processor

The DDL processor translates a schema definition and stores the information into *definition tables*. If the user modifies the schema definition, the DDL processor updates the definition tables and conforms its relevant databases to the new schema. Definition tables contain all the necessary information on schema definitions. Most of the information for construction of the definition tables is directly supplied by the user's schema definition (DDL program). Since the DBMS makes frequent access to these tables for mapping of physical to logical storage and vice versa, the organization of definition tables is important. The definition tables can also serve as a basis for a data dictionary. The following are major definition tables:

1. Schema definition table
2. Record definition table
3. Attribute definition table
4. Link definition table
5. Constraint definition table
6. View definition table

Volatile records and links exist only during a single session or run. The definitions of such volatile objects are kept only during the period of their existence.

5.3.2 Schema Definition

For each user or user group, we create a schema directory which consists of at least two entries: a schema name and a pointer to a schema definition table. In an actual implementation, the second entry might be the name of a file which contains all the definition tables. The schema definition table is composed of the following entries for each schema:

1. Number of record types contained in the schema
2. Number of link types contained in the schema
3. Number of all the attributes in the schema
4. Number of constraint definitions
5. Number of view definitions

Only the number of record types in a schema is stored in the schema definition table. Actual record type definitions are stored in a record definition table. In this way, we can also easily accommodate changes in a record type definition, and additions/deletions of record type definitions. Similar concerns apply for the other definition tables. Figure 5.3 illustrates how the several tables are interrelated.

5.3.3 Record Definition

The record definition table has the following entries for each record type:

1. Record type name
2. Record length
3. Pointer to a record occurrence file (file name)
4. Physical clustering attributes
5. Unique key attributes
6. Search key attributes
7. Number of attributes
8. Pointer to an attribute definition table
9. Number of incident link types
10. Pointers to incident link type lists

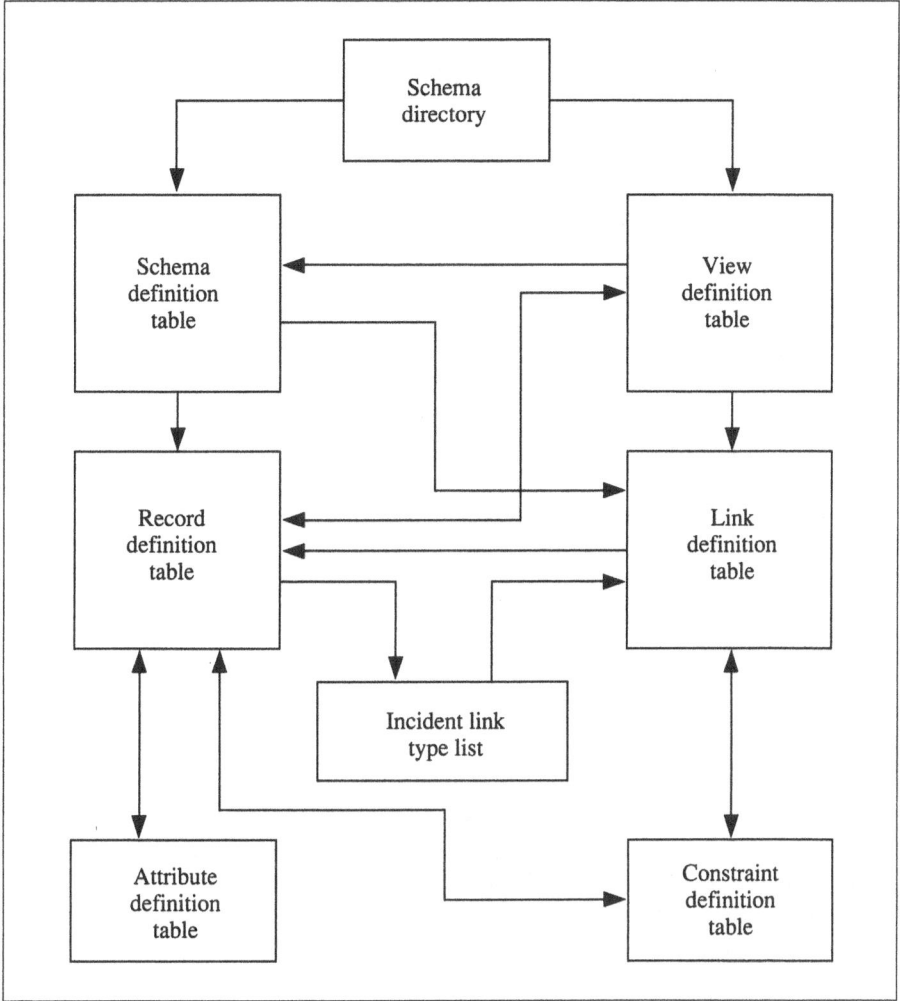

Fig. 5.3. Definition tables

11. Number of constraint definitions
12. Pointer to a constraint definition table

Pointers mentioned in this chapter are usually indices to other tables.

A file into which the DBMS stores actual record occurrences is called a *record occurrence file*. The physical clustering attributes specify in what order, record occurrences are placed in this file. If a unique key is defined for a record type, then its record occurrences are uniquely identified by the key. The search key attributes are those attributes which are provided with a fast access mechanism (indices). The incident link list is simply a list containing pointers to the link definition table. This list is used to identify link types that are incident to a given record type. There are two types of incident link types depending on whether the record type serves as an initial node or as a terminal node.

5.3.4 Attribute Definition

The attribute definition table contains the following information for each attribute:

1. Attribute name
2. Data type
3. Length
4. Access path information (key or not)

5.3.5 Link Definition

A link definition table is composed of the following entries:

1. Link type name
2. Kind of link types (real or virtual)
3. Pointer to an initial node record type in the record definition table
4. Pointer to a terminal node record type in the record definition table
5. Pointer to a link occurrence file (for real link types)
6. Number of constraint definitions (for real link types)
7. Pointer to a constraint definition table (for real link types)
8. Linking condition (for virtual link types)

The *link occurrence* file is a file for storing the occurrences of a link type.

5.3.6 Constraints, Views, and Evolution of Schemas

Definitions of constraints, views, and schema changes are operational; the definitions have close correspondence with DML statements. A constraint definition is translated into a DML statement (actually a sequence of run-time procedures) at definition time and the name of the object program is stored in the constraint definition table. The program itself can be stored in a separate file. It is called by the run-time system or the query processor whenever the storage operation is executed on the associated record or link type. Since an attribute is not a unit of storage, we do not associate constraint definitions with attribute definitions, but rather with record type definitions.

A view definition is also translated into a set of DML statements. The query modification approach proposed by Stonebraker et al. [69] is employed to implement the view facility. That is, DML statements against a view are modified to include the DML statements for the construction of the view.

When a schema is changed after the database is loaded, the DBMS must update not only the schema definition but also the databases to make them conform to the updated schema definition. The user specifies this process in terms of DML statements.

5.4 Run-time System

5.4.1 Overview of Query Evaluation

We show a global picture of query evaluation by informally describing the execution of a few typical DML statements. Consider the following DML statement which selects record occurrences of record type R3 qualified by a path expression:

$$\text{select record RESULT} := \text{R3 [path R1[P1]} \rightarrow /\text{L1}/ \rightarrow$$
$$\text{R2[P2]} \rightarrow /\text{L2}/ \rightarrow \text{R3[P3]]}$$

where P1, P2, and P3 are some expressions qualifying record types R1, R2, and R3, respectively. P1, P2, and P3 can be an intra-record restriction or a path expression. Path expressions are recursively evaluated if they are nested. We can summarize the query evaluation procedure as follows:

1 Evaluate P1, creating $\{(r1)\}$
2. Traverse L1, creating $\{(r2)\}$
3. Evaluate P2, restricting $\{(r2)\}$
4. Traverse L2, creating $\{(r3)\}$
5. Evaluate P3, restricting $\{(r3)\}$
6. Fetch the record occurrences whose URIs are in $\{(r3)\}$

where (ri) stands for a URI-tuple which is composed of a URI for record type Ri. Note that the URI-tuples carry sufficient information for selecting record occurrences.

Another example illustrates the evaluation of an inter-record restriction. Suppose we have:

$$\text{select record RESULT} := \text{R3[path R1[P1]} \rightarrow /\text{L1}/ \rightarrow$$
$$\text{R2[P2]} \rightarrow /\text{L2}/ \rightarrow \text{R3[P3]: P4(R1, R3)]}$$

where P4 is an inter-record restriction of R1 and R3.

Its execution sequence is:

1. Evaluate P1, creating $\{(r1)\}$
2. Traverse L1, creating $\{(r1, r2)\}$
3. Evaluate P2, restricting $\{(r1, r2)\}$
4. Traverse L2, creating $\{(r1, r3)\}$
5. Evaluate P3, restricting $\{(r1, r3)\}$
6. Evaluate P4, creating $\{(r3)\}$
7. Fetch the record occurrences whose URIs are in $\{(r3)\}$

Note how record list types change. The precompiler specifies these record list types by keeping track of target record types and record types appearing in inter-record restrictions.

Record occurrences are fetched only if they are not in the working space. In many cases, we can avoid record fetches by using indices and links. As we will describe later, run-time procedures keep track of the contents of the buffer in order to minimize the number of record fetches. Global query optimization is avoided in our design. Instead of modifying a query into an optimized form, we issue warning messages whenever the precompiler or the query processor detects possible ineffi-ciency in evaluating queries. Because of this, the implementation of GDL is rather straightforward. This strategy encourages and assists a user to formulate queries that can be evaluated effectively.

5.4.2 Run-time Data Structures

One of our goals in designing run-time data structures is the effective management of working space for query computation. To execute a single elementary data operation, we need at most:

1. Three storage buffers to hold URI-tuples (two for input operands and one for a result operand)
2. Two storage buffers to hold record occurrences for value comparison

Let us call the first type of storage *URI-arrays* and the second type of storage *record-arrays*. A URI-array holds a record list type. The dimension of a URI-array changes from one elementary operation to another because the record list type which the URI-array represents changes. Also note that some URI-arrays must be saved to handle nested expressions. Record-arrays are used only when values of record occurrences must be fetched or when query evaluation is more efficient when working directly on record occurrences.

Our proposed data structures for run-time are given in Fig. 5.4. There are three stacks to hold URI-arrays. We call them *URI-stacks*. There are two small stacks to indicate current operand URI-array(s) and to keep track of where intermediate results are stored. These two stacks are called the *operand-display-stack* and the *record-list-display-stack*, respectively. As execution of a query proceeds, we assign one of the available URI-stacks to a URI-array at run-time. The assignment algorithm is given in Sect. 5.3.4.

The operand-display-stack has at most three slots, each of which contains:

1. URI-stack identifier
2. Position where a URI-array starts in the stack
3. Degree of the URI-tuple

The record-list-display-stack contains the same information as the above for each URI-array (record list type) pushed onto one of the URI-stacks. There are also two record-stacks and a record-display-stack. A record-stack contains one or more record-arrays, and the record-display-stack specifies the contents of the record-stacks. This information is utilized to minimize the number of record fetches. Each entry of this stack is comprised of:

1. Record-stack identifier
2. Position where a record-array starts in the stack
3. Record length

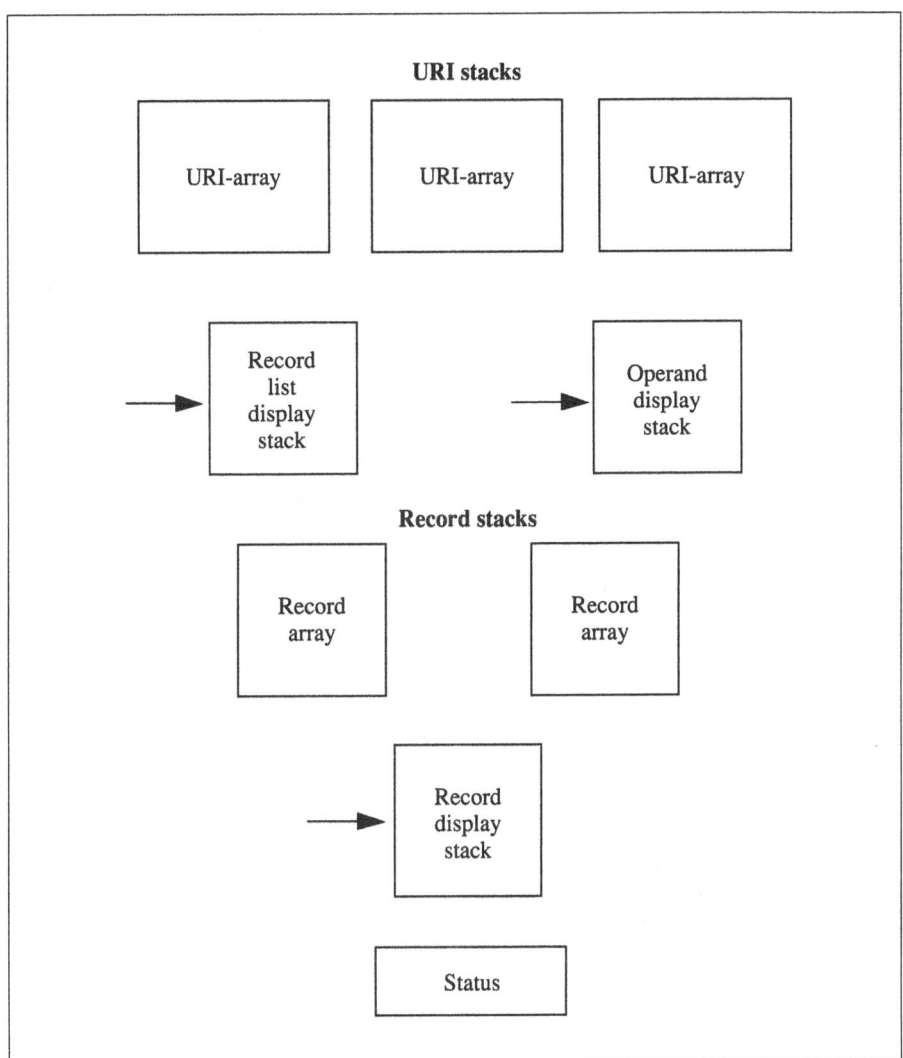

Fig. 5.4. Major data structures of run-time system

If both record-stacks have no more unused space, then new record occurrences are circularly superposed on the used space.

5.4.3 Run-time Procedures

A list of GDL run-time procedures which the precompiler sees is given in Fig. 5.5. We call them the *first-level run-time procedures*. Most of the Elementary Data Operations described in Chap. 3 are readily implemented as run-time procedures of the first level. A restriction operation may be decomposed into two cases: a restric-

— Record restriction:	IRST, XRST
— Record formation:	PROJ, FETCH
— Link traversal:	EXT, NEGEXT, NUM, TRN
— Link creation:	LNKCRT
— Set manipulation:	UNI, INTS, DIF
— Storage manipulation:	RADD, RDEL, LADD, LDEL
— Sequencing operation:	PUSH, POP

Fig. 5.5. Run-time procedures of the first level

tion involving only a single record type and a restriction involving two record types. Run-time procedure IRST (XRST) executes an intra-record expression (an inter-record expression) described in Chap. 4. Run-time procedures for storage operations deal with a set of occurrences rather than an individual occurrence. No set operations can be executed directly on stored databases. The record list projection operation is incorporated into other data operations.

PUSH and POP are run-time procedures which do not have corresponding operations in Elementary Data Operations because these are sequencing operations. They handle the bookkeeping for nested expressions. Another procedure which does not appear in Elementary Data Operations is FETCH. It brings in record occurrences of a given record type whose URIs are stored in one of the URI-stacks but not in the record-stacks.

Figure 5.6 gives an example of translation for a select-record statement. The parameter values of the run-time procedures are symbolically represented in the figure, although they are numerical values in an actual environment. Appendix B contains descriptions of run-time procedures.

Figure 5.7 gives another example to illustrate how a nested path expression is executed in terms of a sequence of run-time procedures. The PUSH procedure is called whenever a nested path expression is encountered. It keeps track of where an intermediate result (a resultant URI-array) is stored, by updating the display stacks and a URI-stack pointer. After evaluating the inner expression, the POP procedure restores the previous result. Then, we call the INTS procedure to make the intersection of the two lists.

The first-level run-time procedures share many procedures which perform smaller functions. We call them the *second-level run-time procedures*. Those functions are classified into:

1. Retrieval of
   a) Records — GETREC
   b) Links — GETLNK
   c) Indices — GETIDX

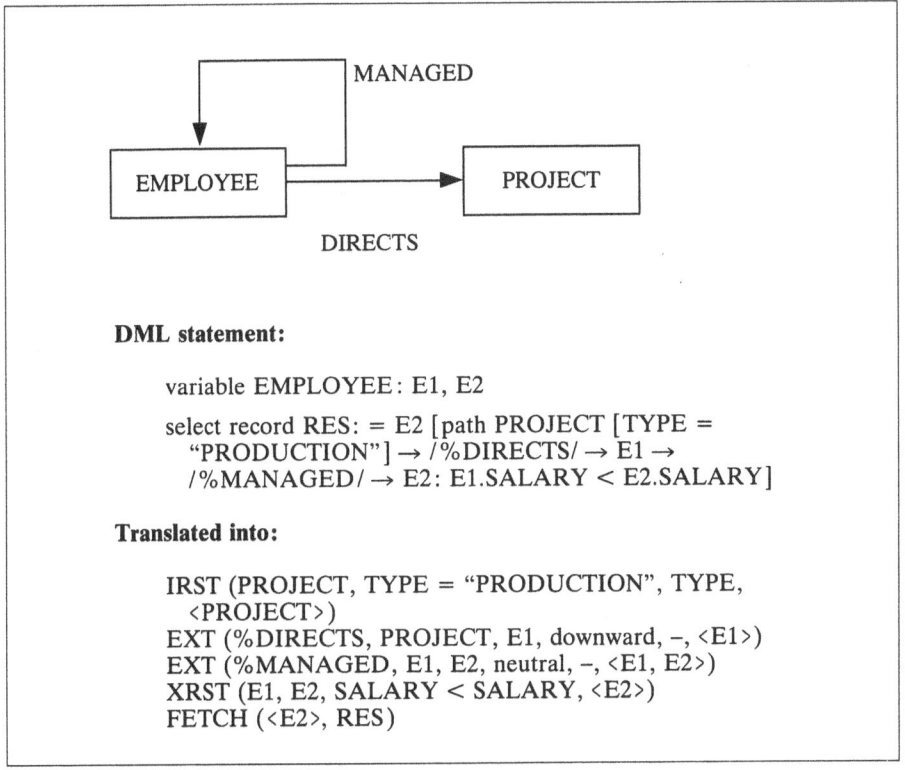

DML statement:

    variable EMPLOYEE: E1, E2

    select record RES: = E2 [path PROJECT [TYPE =
        "PRODUCTION"] → /%DIRECTS/ → E1 →
        /%MANAGED/ → E2: E1.SALARY < E2.SALARY]

Translated into:

    IRST (PROJECT, TYPE = "PRODUCTION", TYPE,
        ⟨PROJECT⟩)
    EXT (%DIRECTS, PROJECT, E1, downward, –, ⟨E1⟩)
    EXT (%MANAGED, E1, E2, neutral, –, ⟨E1, E2⟩)
    XRST (E1, E2, SALARY < SALARY, ⟨E2⟩)
    FETCH (⟨E2⟩, RES)

Fig. 5.6. Example of DML translation

2. Storage manipulation (add and delete) of
   a) Records — ADDREC, DELREC
   b) Links — ADDLNK, DELLNK
   c) Index — ADDIDX, DELIDX
3. Working space manipulation of
   a) URI-stacks — ASGNRL, DELRL
   b) Record-stacks — ASGNREC
4. Record list projection — RLPROJ
5. Other operations
   a) Grouping — GROUP
   b) Sorting — SORT

Retrieval and storage manipulation depend heavily on access paths, which are discussed in Sect. 5.6. The working space assignment has an important bearing on performance. Procedure ASGNREC tries to minimize the number of record re-fetches. If a record type in the record-stack appears in a resultant record list type, we often need it later. We say that the record type is *useful*. As long as there is enough space, we want to keep it in the record-stack. We do not know in advance,

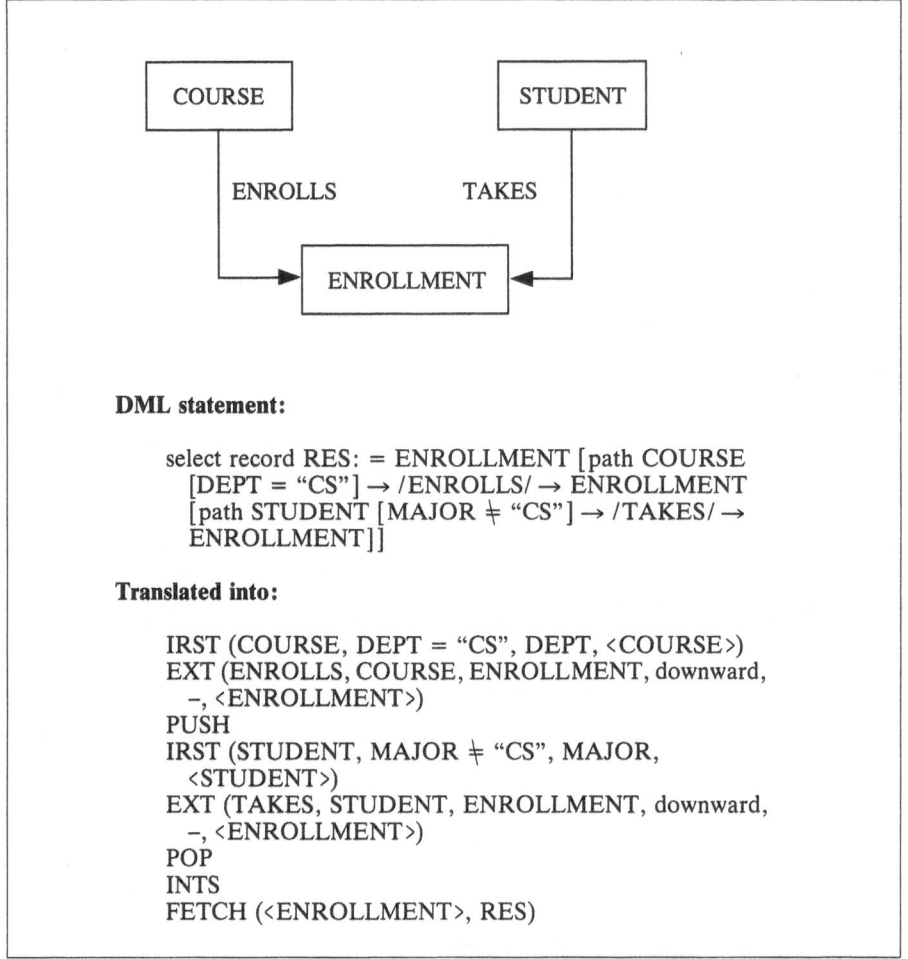

DML statement:

> select record RES: = ENROLLMENT [path COURSE
> [DEPT = "CS"] → /ENROLLS/ → ENROLLMENT
> [path STUDENT [MAJOR ≠ "CS"] → /TAKES/ →
> ENROLLMENT]]

Translated into:

> IRST (COURSE, DEPT = "CS", DEPT, <COURSE>)
> EXT (ENROLLS, COURSE, ENROLLMENT, downward,
>   −, <ENROLLMENT>)
> PUSH
> IRST (STUDENT, MAJOR ≠ "CS", MAJOR,
>   <STUDENT>)
> EXT (TAKES, STUDENT, ENROLLMENT, downward,
>   −, <ENROLLMENT>)
> POP
> INTS
> FETCH (<ENROLLMENT>, RES)

Fig. 5.7. Another example of DML translation

however, the number of record occurrences which must be stored in the record buffer to complete a given operation. We use a simple algorithm to solve this problem. First, we always keep the useful record types. If we run out of space, we overwrite the occurrences of the useful record types that are not used in the current operation, and record the fact in the record-display-stack, i.e., an LRU algorithm.

It is possible for the precompiler to make the assignment of URI-stacks and record-stacks to the storage for Elementary Data Operations. In this case, however, the precompiler has no means of knowing the sizes of remaining working spaces, which may lead to inefficient management of working spaces.

5.5 DML Precompiler

The precompiler has the following major functions:

1. Translate DML statements into a set of data declaration statements and a sequence of run-time procedure call statements
2. Check errors and issue error messages if errors are detected
3. Issue warning messages upon detection of possible inefficiencies in query evaluation

An inter-record restriction operation is executed at the end of the associated path expression. We need to keep track of which record types are involved in inter-record restrictions.

Figure 5.8 gives the major data structures of the DML at translation-time, except those for parsing. In translating a DML statement, it is rather straightforward to find a proper sequence of run-time procedures. The target code generated textually follows the structure of the DML statement. Figure 5.9 illustrates a conceptual

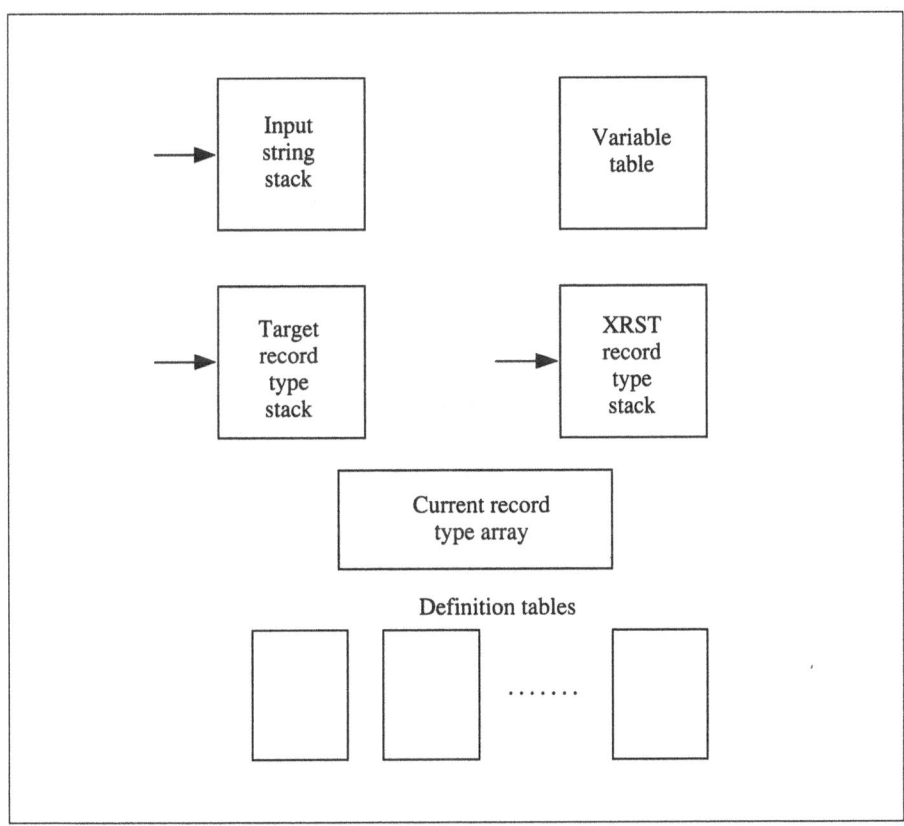

Fig. 5.8. Major data structures of precompiler

```
        procedure evalrec (EXP: selection expression)
    begin
        case expression-type of

        no qualification : ;

        intra record restriction
                    : eval-irst;
                        /* write IRST (IRST-EXP), etc. */

        path expression : /* R1(P1) → /L1/ → R2 → ....
                            : XRST-EXP             */

            begin

                push; /* previous result */

                evalrec (R1);

                i: = 1;

                while not end-of-path do
                    begin
                        evallink (Li);
                        /* write EXT (Li, ...), etc. */
                        evalrec (Ri + 1);
                        i: = i + 1;

                    end;

                if exist-xrst then eval-xrst;
                    /* write XRST (XRST-EXP), etc. */

                pop;

                eval-intersection;
                        /* write INTS */

            end

    end
```

Fig. 5.9. Algorithm for translation of selection expressions

algorithm for translating the main part of a selection expression. The algorithm does not include the translation of parentheses and set operations.

Generating proper parameters for the procedures requires more work. The system must know the context: the target record types, the record types involved in inter-record restrictions, and the record list type of the result from the last operation. We call these three types of information *context-determining factors*. The first two factors must be saved when the processing of nested path expressions or set operations causes the query evaluation flow control to branch out. The two stacks in Fig. 5.8 (target record-stack and record restriction stack) are used for this purpose. After evaluating the nested path expressions or set operations, the system must restore the previous context by updating those stacks.

The precompiler selects access paths by looking up definition tables. In general, a query represented in GDL will execute with reasonable efficiency because the query representation itself tells the system which access paths to use. One possible source for poor performance lies in intra-record restrictions. If every attribute appearing in an intra-record restriction is neither a primary key nor a search key, then the system must get all the record occurrences and check their values. Unless the number of the record occurrences is small, this will cause poor performance. When the precompiler detects this case, then it produces a warning message.

5.6 Access Paths and Other Environment-Dependent Factors

We have up to this point been as abstract as possible so that the system design is independent of execution environment details. In this section, we discuss how the design can be mapped onto an actual environment. Major factors which affect more detailed design are:

1. Available file structures and file management system supported by a given operating system
2. Target/host languages into which user's programs are translated
3. Storage management facilities of a given operating system

The file structure is the major determining factor for the performance of the DBMS. Thus, our discussion here is concentrated on this subject. The target or host language obviously affects data structures, procedure calls, program structures, etc. Since a DBMS is a rather complex system, a language which supports structured programming is desirable. Locality of storage is also important to satisfactory system performance, because the DBMS needs big working spaces. A storage management system that effectively supports locality will give better performance.

We may use different file structures to store different types of information. Table 5.1 gives one proposal for file type assignment. To store table definitions, it is convenient to have two types of file:

1. A schema directory file for each user, or one centralized schema directory file
2. For each schema, a file which contains all the definition tables and lists for the schema

Table 5.1. Suggested file structures

Object stored in a file	File structure
Schema directory	Hash, B-tree, B*-tree, indexed sequential
Definition tables	Sequential
Record occurrence file	B-tree, B*-tree, indexed sequential, hash
Link occurrence file	B-tree, B*-tree, indexed sequential
Key (access path) file	B-tree, B*-tree, indexed sequential

The schema directory can use almost any random access file structure. The reason why we put the rest of definitions for a schema in a single file is that the DBMS needs to access most of the information in this file when translating GDL statements. We therefore load the full definition tables for a schema all together. A sequential file structure is adequate for this file.

To select an appropriate structure for a given file, we need to know its access patterns. It is common to access a record occurrence file both randomly and sequentially. It is also common to retrieve record occurrences by using comparison operators such as > and < . Thus, indexed sequential, B-tree or B*-tree type file organizations are appropriate for record occurrences. A hashed file organization performs well if the file is accessed only randomly. A link occurrence file contains pairs of URI-tuples. We can choose either a B-tree, B*-tree or indexed sequential file structure for a link occurrence file. Since the data structure of the link occurrence file does not differ from one link type to another, we can store multiple link types in a single physical file.

A key file provides a secondary access path to the record occurrence file. It might use simple inversion for a single attribute or more sophisticated key access for a combination of attributes. A link occurrence file is similar to a record occurrence file with respect to file structure selection.

The final decision may depend on the application of the DBMS. Although each object type may favor different file structures, the DBMS may be implemented with fewer file structures for uniformity and overall efficiency. B-tree, B*-tree or indexed sequential file structure may be a reasonable choice if we have only a single structure for record occurrence, link occurrence and key files.

5.7 Query Processor

The function of a query processor is more or less a union of the functions of a precompiler and a run-time system. Problems particular to the query processor are formatting and buffer storage for record occurrences. Since the buffer is invisible to the user, the query processor must reserve a common buffer that is used for any record type, and must interpret it for each query. If the DBMS allows many data types as attributes, buffer handling becomes more cumbersome.

6. A Comparison of Access Path Strategies

6.1 Introduction

This chapter compares the performances of a database management system based upon GDM and a DBMS based on the relational data model in terms of effective use of access paths in query processing. Performance evaluation requires the specification of storage structures, query-processing algorithms, states of schemas, and the workload of queries to be processed. The specification of storage structures is given in terms of definitions for record, index, and link storage. The state of the schema is given in terms of a set of parameters such as number of occurrences, index selection, and selectivity on attributes. The workload is a set of one-, two-, and three-variable queries. Yao's [80] cost model has embedded definition of query-processing algorithms and establishes the relationships between storage structures, schema states, and query specifications. Yao's cost model uses accesses to external storage as its cost metric. We have extended Yao's cost model to include the algorithms necessary for processing queries against GDM.

Design and evaluation of query-processing algorithms has been a major research topic in the implementation of relational database management systems. The problem arises from the fact that relationships between record types (relations) are implicitly represented by values. The cost of joins becomes dependent on hidden access paths.

The query optimization problem has been investigated at several levels and angles, from optimization of a single isolated database operation to global optimization of multiple queries. We give here a brief summary of some significant papers and in particular mention those papers which contain comparisons of performance of access strategies.

Yao [78] and Astrahan et al. [2] studied the evaluation algorithms of a restriction operation. Gotlieb [35] investigated join algorithms and evaluated their costs. Blasgen and Eswaran [9] proposed a model of storage and access to a relational system and compared the costs of possible query evaluation algorithms of a two-variable query by using their model. Yao [79, 80] synthesized a model for database storage and access which encompasses most query-processing algorithms in the relational model. Yao classified algorithms for the evaluation of two-variable queries in the relational system and derived formulae to compute the costs of these algorithms. Rosenthal and Reiner [57] have proposed a two-level access cost model which consists of the specification of a join sequence and the specification of an access path of eacn join. Astrahan and Kim [4] and Chamberlin et al. [14] have given the actual cost for evaluation of one- and two-variable queries executed in System R.

Wong and Youssefi [76, 81] have proposed and evaluated decomposition strategies for multi-variable queries. Selinger et al. [62] described a method of access path selection for the multi-variable query used in System R. Nested queries in SQL were analyzed by Kim [46]. Finkelstein [32] proposed techniques to eliminate the repetitive evaluation of common expressions in multiple queries in a given program.

Yao's model describes query evaluation algorithms in an abstract but rather detailed manner. The algorithms are mapped to references to external storage through assignment of values, indices, and links to storage structures. It can thus be applied to query evaluation in a variety of data models. The storage structures considered in this model are, however, limited; for example, the model does not include links which are not embedded in record files. We extend Yao's model to incorporate GDM link traversal operations. A few modifications are also made for the sake of increased accuracy of representation. Using this extended model (see Sect. 6.2), we compare the performance of GDM-based access strategies with some of those proposed and/or implemented for relational systems.

Yao's model assumes that secondary storage is organized in pages. The cost of each algorithm is computed in terms of the number of page accesses required to process a query, given the specification of the schema state. Queries with three or more variables must be decomposed by some other techniques [76, 9] before being evaluated in this model.

The next section describes the extended model of query evaluation algorithms and the assumed storage structures. The workload includes three types of queries. Section 6.3 contains the comparisons of GDM-based and relational-based systems for these three types of queries. The final section evaluates these results.

6.2 An Extension of Yao's Cost Model for Query Evaluation Algorithms

Query evaluation algorithms differ in the sequences of basic operations such as restriction, join, record access, and projection, and in the access paths used to execute these operations. The storage structures considered in our model are as follows:

1. Record storage. Record occurrences are stored in flat files (record files).
2. Indexes. An index consists of a tree structure file (index tree file) and a flat file (index pointer file). The first file contains pairs consisting of a value and a pointer. The second file contains pointers.
3. Embedded link storage. The pointers to link record occurrences are embedded in record files. Parent-to-child and child-to-parent relationships are both represented.
4. Independent link storage which stores link occurrences in files independent from record files. These files are organized in a tree structure file (link tree file) and a flat file (link pointer file) containing terminal node occurrences similar to the structure of indices.

The first three structures are included in Yao's model; the structure of independent link storage is our extension to his model. The traversal of real link types in GDL uses this independent link storage. The traversal of virtual link types in GDL uses indices (just as is the case in the relational data model). Note that the pointers mentioned here correspond to URIs in our implementation.

The way each storage structure is utilized for query processing is not necessarily fixed to one pattern. For example, an index structure can be used for a restriction by traversing the index tree, or for a join by directly scanning the pointer (URI) files. Table 6.1 gives a summary of the operations which require, or may require, secondary storage accesses.

The cost model of query evaluation except for the accesses to link storage defined by Yao is given in terms of the access operations of Table 6.1. The cost of each of these access operations is determined by the parameters in Table 6.2 which specify characteristics of structures and states of the schema. In this section, we extend the cost formulae to include independent link storage access. First let us define the parameters associated with this storage:

– h_i: link fanout which denotes the average number of link occurrences emanating from each occurrence of an initial node record type.
– z_l: tree degree of a link file, i.e., the number of entries in each node.

Using these parameters, the cost for the access to independent link storage can be written:
$$LA(|R_i|, r_{i'}) = r_{i'}(\log_{z_l}(|R_i| \cdot t_i) + h_i/b_l)$$

$|R_i|$ is the number of occurrences of record type R_i. $r_{i'}$ denotes the number of occurrences of the initial node record type to be accessed. t_i is the join selectivity of record type R_i. b_l is the page size of link pointer files which can be used for adjustment of the length of pointers. (Yao's model also uses b for b_l.) The first term of the parenthesized expression is the cost for the search in the link tree file and the

Table 6.1. Summary of operations requiring secondary storage accesses

IA	Index access
LA	Link access
RA	Record access
RS	Scan on a record file
IS	Scan on an index file
LS	Scan on a link file
Lpc	Embedded parent-to-child link access
Lcp	Embedded child-to-parent link access
T	Sorting
P	Projection
J	Join
Jp	Join of pointers
C	Concatenation
Cp	Concatenation of pointers

Table 6.2. Parameters in Cost Model

b	page size of record files
b_l	page size of index/link pointer files
z_i	index tree degree
z_l	link tree degree
$|R_i|$	number of record occurrences
f_i	record length
p_i	number of pages containing the record file
e_i	number of pages in the storage area
s_{ik}	index selectivity of attribute A_{ik} (of record type R_i)
t_i	join selectivity
h_i	link fanout
$d_{ij} = 1$	if R_1 and R_2 are clustered
$\quad = 0$	otherwise
P_{ij}	expected number of page accesses for the child-to-parent access
P_{ji}	expected number of page accesses for the parent-to-child access
p_i	expected number of page accesses for the twin access
$c_{ik} = -1$	if there is no index for attribute A_{ik}
$\quad = 0$	if there is a non-clustering index for A_{ik}
$\quad = 1$	if there is a clustering index for A_{ik}
$dd = 0$	if the primary key is in the projection
$\quad = 1$	otherwise
rr	clustering index selectivity
ee	non-clustering index selectivity
A	set of projection attributes
q	restriction indexing selectivity
q	restriction selectivity
u_k	number of values accessed for attribute A_k

second term is the cost for the access to the link pointer file. The cost for the scan on the link pointer file is:

$$\text{LS}(|R_i|) = |R_i| \cdot t_i \cdot h_i / b_l$$

To treat a real link traversal operation in a manner comparable with a join operation, we assume:

$$h_i = |R_j| \cdot s_{jk}$$

where $|R_j|$ is the number of record occurrences of the terminal node record type R_j and s_{jk} is the selectivity of a join attribute of R_j.

The costs for the operations listed in Table 6.1 are summarized in Fig. 6.1. Also included is the record length H after a projection. Note that IA and Lpc are modified to be more accurate than in Yao's model. The term for the number of accesses in an index tree file in the cost formula for IA is written as $\log_{z_i}(1/s_{ik})$ in the

$$\text{IA}\,(|R_i|) = \sum_{k=1}^{m} u_k\,(\log_{z_i}(1/s_{ik}) + |R_i|\cdot s_{ik}/b_l)$$

$$\text{LA}(|R|) = |R|\cdot(\log_{z_i}(1/t_i) + h_i/b_l)$$

$$\text{RA}(\alpha,\beta) = x + (p_i - x)\cdot\alpha\cdot|R_i|\cdot P_i/p_i$$
$$\text{where } x = p_i(1 - (1 - 1/p_i)^{|R_i|\cdot\beta})$$

if used after restriction:
$$\alpha = rr$$
$$\beta = ee$$

if used after join:
$$\alpha = t_i \qquad \text{if the join has a clustering index}$$
$$\quad = 0 \qquad \text{otherwise}$$
$$\beta = t_i - \alpha$$

if used after restriction and join:
$$\alpha = t_i \qquad \text{if the join has a clustering index}$$
$$\quad = rr \qquad \text{otherwise}$$
$$\beta = ee \qquad \text{if the join has a clustering index}$$
$$\quad = ee.t_i \qquad \text{otherwise}$$

if used for relation scanning:
$$\alpha = 1 \qquad \text{if the scanning index is a clustering index}$$
$$\quad = 0 \qquad \text{otherwise}$$
$$\beta = 1 - \alpha$$

$$\text{RS}(e_i) = e_i$$
$$\text{IS}(|R_i|) = |R_i| \,/\, b_l$$
$$\text{LS}(|R_i|) = |R_i|\cdot t_i\cdot h_i \,/\, b_l$$
$$\text{Lpc}(q) = d_{ij}\cdot|R_j|\cdot t_j\cdot(P_{ji} + (h_j\cdot q - 1)\cdot P_i)$$
$$\quad + (1 - d_{ij})\cdot|R_j|\cdot t_j\cdot(c_{ik}\,(1 + (h_j\cdot q - 1)\cdot P_i)$$
$$\quad + (1 - c_{ik})\cdot h_j\cdot q)$$
where c_{ik} is defined for the join attribute A_{ik}
$$\text{Lcp}(q) = d_{ij}\cdot|R_i|\cdot t_i\cdot q\cdot P_{ij} + (1 - d_{ij})\cdot|R_i|\cdot t_i\cdot q$$
$$\text{T}(|R|,f_i) = 2\cdot(|R|\cdot f_i/b)\cdot\log_n(|R|\cdot f_i/b)$$
$$\text{P}(|R|) = \text{T}(|R|,f_i) + (dd/s_{ik})\cdot\text{T}(|R|\cdot s_{ik}, f_i) \quad \text{applicable before SORT}$$
$$\text{P}_1(|R|) = (1/s_{ik})\cdot\text{T}(|R|\cdot s_{ik}, f_i) \quad \text{applicable after SORT}$$
$$\text{H}(|R|) = \text{MIN}\,(|R|;\, \prod_{A_k\in A}(1/s_{ik})) \quad \text{record length after projection}$$

$$\text{J}(|R|,f_i) = |R|\cdot f_i \,/\, b$$
$$\text{Jp}(|R|) = |R| \,/\, b_l$$
$$\text{C}(|R|,f_i) = |R|\cdot f_i \,/\, b$$
$$\text{Cp}(|R|) = |R|\cdot t_i\cdot h_i \,/\, b_l$$

Fig. 6.1. Cost model of query evaluation

extended model. Yao uses $|R_i|$ in the place of $(1/s_{ik})$. The latter is, however, more accurate than the former as the number of distinct values for a given attribute. As the number of child pointers in the cost formula for Lpc, we used h_j instead of $|R_i| \cdot t_i$. Yao's formula assumes that every occurrence of a parent record type is (if the occurrence is ever selected for the join operation) connected to all the occurrences of the child record type that are selected for the join operation. This assumption means that, for example, if a course is taken by at least one student, then this course is taken by all the students who take at least one course.

Schkolnick's [61] analysis on the expected numbers of page accesses associated with the record storage and the embedded link storage (i.e., P_{ij}, P_{ji} and P_i) is used for the derivation of RA, Lpc and Lcp. The cost for sorting is computed for an n-way sort-merge algorithm [47, 10]. The total cost of a query evaluation algorithm will be computed by summing up the cost of each storage operation generated by the execution of the algorithms.

6.3 Costs of Query Evaluation Algorithms

A comparison of a GDM-based system with a relational-based system with respect to access path strategies is performed for three types of queries:

1. One-variable query
2. Two-variable query
3. Three-variable query

We are not concerned here with details of syntax of data languages. Therefore, the queries compared here are diagrammatically expressed. Query algorithms are also described by diagrams, following the notation used by Yao. The basic operations in Table 6.1 and other supporting operations in Table 6.3 are possible components of query evaluation algorithms. Each algorithm is defined by selection of a sequence of these operations.

6.3.1 One-Variable Queries

Evaluation of one-variable queries is straightforward. The diagram of a one-variable query is given in Fig. 6.2. It states "select record occurrences that satisfy a given restriction predicate for record type R_1 and project them on attribute A_1." The rectangle with label R_1 denotes a record type R_1.

Table 6.3. Supporting operations for query evaluation

RF	restriction filter
JF	join filter
LF	link filter
I	intersection

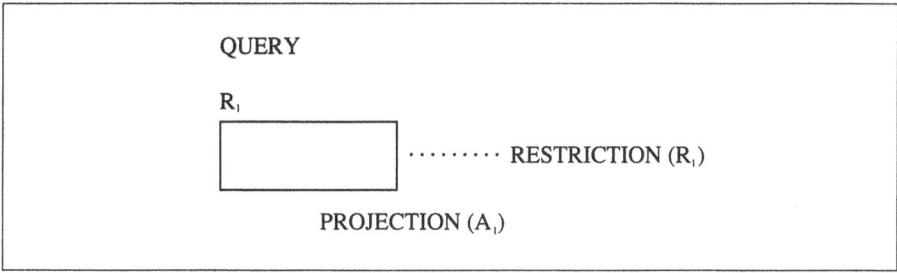

Fig. 6.2. One-variable query

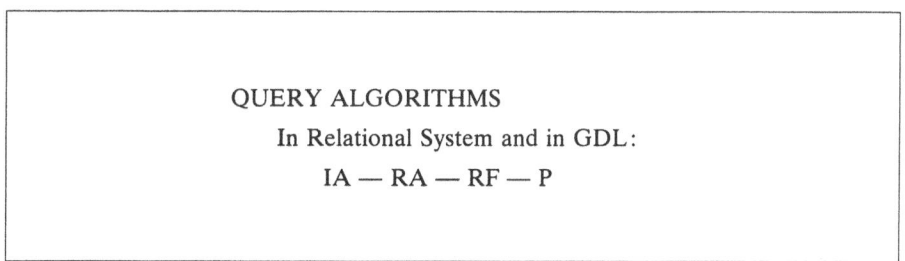

Fig. 6.3. Algorithms for one-variable queries

The evaluation algorithms are given in Fig. 6.3. If there exist one or more indexes on the attributes in the restriction predicate, the indexes are first accessed to get pointers. The record occurrences are accessed using these pointers. The restriction filter RF executes the rest of the expression of the restriction predicate, namely, the restriction on the attributes that have no indexes. RF does not, however, require access to secondary storage. P is a projection operation.

The evaluation of one-variable queries is basically identical both in the relational system and in GDL. Its cost is expressed as:

$$COST(|R_1|) = IA(|R_1|) + RA(rr, ee)$$

6.3.2 Two-Variable Queries

The evaluation algorithms for two-variable queries in the relational system have been extensively studied by Yao [80]. He classified algorithms for evaluating a single record type into seven classes in terms of sequences of the three basic operations—restriction, join, and record access. Within a class, algorithms differ upon where projection and concatenation operations take place. These differences within a class define versions of a class. Algorithms are called by numbers where the first and second digits denote the class and version, respectively. The first version of each class is used for comparison in this chapter. Figure 6.4 summarizes the structure of these algorithms. Evaluation algorithms for two-variable queries are in

CLASS 11:

IA — RA — RF — T — JF — C — P

CLASS 21:

IS — JF — RA — RF — C — P

CLASS 31:

IA ——————┐
                    ├— I — RA — RF — C — P
IS — JF ———┘

CLASS 41:

RS — RF — T — JF — C — P

or

IS — RA — RF — T — JF — C — P

CLASS 51:

RS — T — JF — RF — C — P

or

IS — RA — T — JF — RF — C — P

CLASS 61:

↓
Lpc — RF — C — P

or

↓
Lcp — RF — C — P

CLASS 71:

        ↓
IA — I — Lpc — RF — C — P

or

        ↓
IA — I — Lcp — RF — C — P

Fig. 6.4. Query evaluation algorithms classified by Yao

turn described by a pair of algorithms, e.g., 21/31. The same algorithm can be used for two variables such as 31/31 and 41/41. Certain combinations using Lpc and Lcp (e.g., 21/61 and 31/61) are not conceptually possible because Lpc and Lcp require, prior to their execution, the pointers to be accessed.

Yao's analysis distinguishes 31 basic types of algorithms, each of which has many· versions. With the inclusion of the independent link storage, the number of algorithms is in the hundreds. Furthermore, the algorithms actually implemented

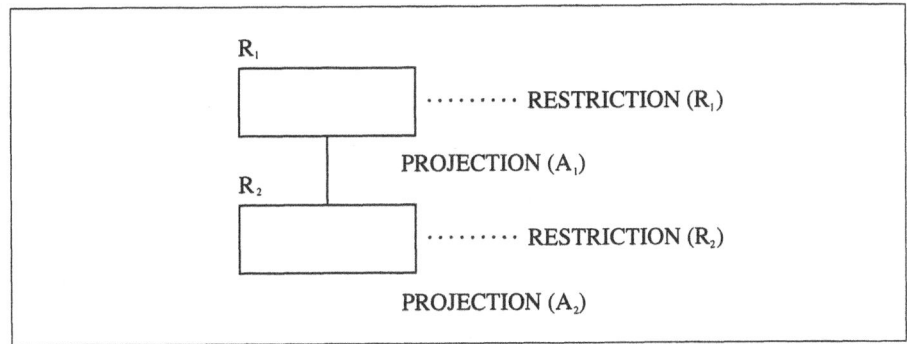

Fig. 6.5. Two-variable query

are often variants of these algorithms. It is impossible to analyze exhaustively all the algorithms for all the possible combinations of queries and schema states. We compare the costs for several realistic cases. Figure 6.5 shows a two-variable query to be analyzed.

Most of the algorithms discussed by Yao can be implemented in GDL—the exceptions are those algorithms which use Lpc and Lcp operations, because we do not support embedded link storage. The basic GDL algorithms which use independent link storage are summarized in Fig. 6.6. R_1 and R_2 in the figure are assumed to be the initial node record type and the terminal node record type of a given link type, respectively.

The cost formulae for GDL algorithms where both join and restriction indexes are not clustered are summarized in Fig. 6.7. The values of parameters are listed in Tables 6.4 and 6.5. In these tables, s_{ik} for a restriction attribute A_{ik} is denoted by s_i since there is only one restriction attribute considered. c_j is similarly defined for the index for a join attribute. The values are selected so as to be realistic; they are also often seen in the literature on performance of query processing. Rothnie's feedback effects are taken into consideration in terms of $F(q_j)$ in the formulae [58, 80]. The parameters are *not* necessarily *independent*. The following parameters are important in displaying the effects of access path strategies on execution cost:

1. Index selectivities: s_1, s_2
2. Join selectivities: t_1, t_2
3. Link fanout: h_1, h_2
4. Whether there exist indexes on restriction and join attributes or not

In the following case studies, we change only these parameters. We also assume:

- All the indexes on restriction and join attributes, if any, are non-clustered.
- Every query has only one restriction attribute and one value to be accessed, e.g., $R_i[A_{ik} = \text{"value"}]$.
- No clustering among record types.

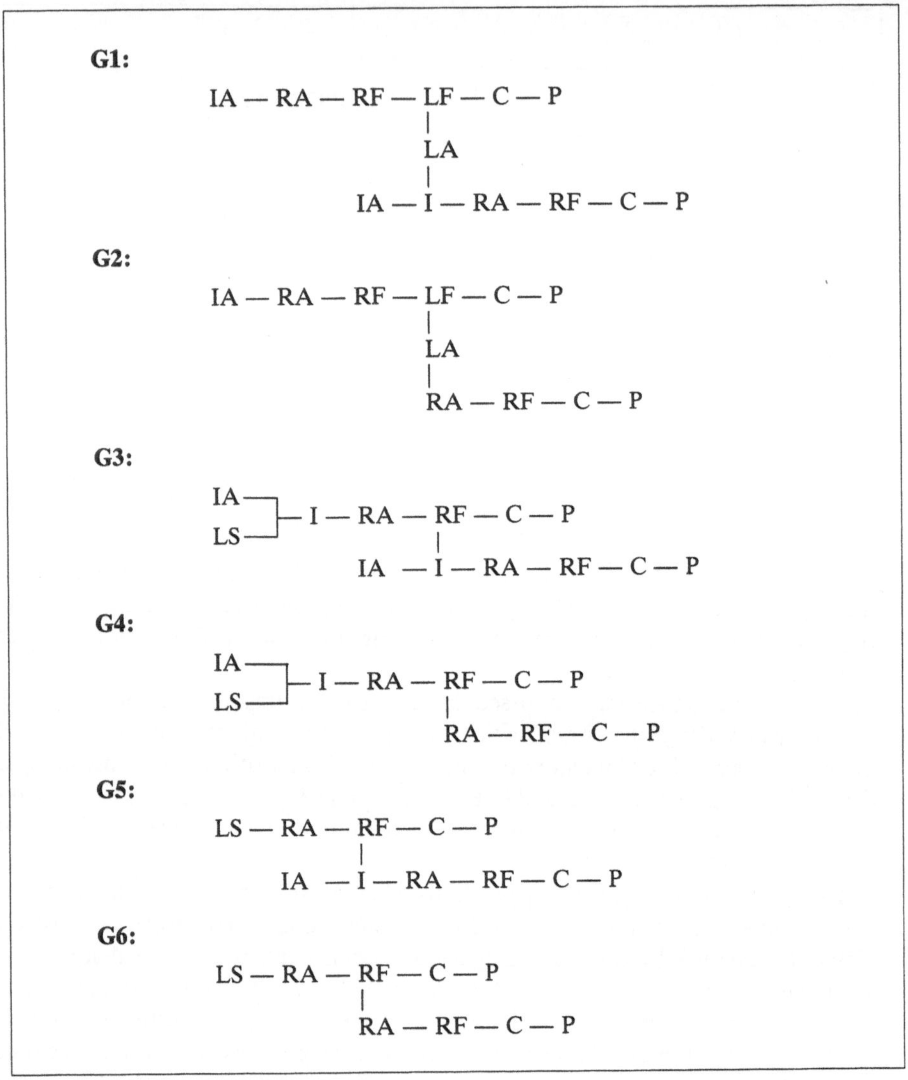

G1:

$$IA - RA - RF - LF - C - P$$
$$|$$
$$LA$$
$$|$$
$$IA - I - RA - RF - C - P$$

G2:

$$IA - RA - RF - LF - C - P$$
$$|$$
$$LA$$
$$|$$
$$RA - RF - C - P$$

G3:

$$IA$$
$$ \rbrace - I - RA - RF - C - P$$
$$LS$$
$$|$$
$$IA - I - RA - RF - C - P$$

G4:

$$IA$$
$$ \rbrace - I - RA - RF - C - P$$
$$LS$$
$$|$$
$$RA - RF - C - P$$

G5:

$$LS - RA - RF - C - P$$
$$|$$
$$IA - I - RA - RF - C - P$$

G6:

$$LS - RA - RF - C - P$$
$$|$$
$$RA - RF - C - P$$

Fig. 6.6 GDL query evaluation algorithms using a real link type

These assumptions lead to:

$$d_{ij} = 0$$
$$c_i \neq 1$$
$$c_j \neq 1$$
$$rr_i = 0$$
$$ee_i = s_i = q_i = \underline{q}_i$$

Definitions:

$r_{i'} = r_i \cdot q_i$

$r_{i''} = r_{i'} \cdot t_i$

$r_{i'''} = r_{i''} \cdot F(q_j)$

$F(q_j) = 1 - (1 - 1 / q_j)^{h_j}$

Assumptions:

$d_{ij} = 0$

$c_i \neq 1$

$c_j \neq 1$

$rr_t = 0$

$ee_t = s_i = q_i = q_i$

Costs:

$\text{COST}_{G1} =$
$$IA(|R_1|) + RA(0,s_1) + LA(r_{1'}) + C(r_{1''},f_1) + IA(|R_2|) +$$
$$RA(0, s_2 \cdot t_2 \cdot F(s_1 \cdot t_1)) + C(r_{2'''},f_2)$$

$\text{COST}_{G2} =$
$$IA(|R_1|) + RA(0,s_1) + LA(r_{1'}) + C(r_{1''},f_1) +$$
$$RA(0,t_2 \cdot F(s_1,t_1)) + C(r_{2'''},f_2)$$

$\text{COST}_{G3} =$
$$IA(|R_1|) + LS(|R_1| \cdot t_1) + RA(0,s_1) + C(r_{1''},f_1) + IA(|R_2|)$$
$$+ RA(0,s_2 \cdot t_2 \cdot F(s_1,t_1))) + C(r_{2'''},f_2)$$

$\text{COST}_{G4} =$
$$IA(|R_1|) + LS(|R_1| \cdot t_1) + RA(0,s_1) + C(r_{1''},f_1) +$$
$$RA(0,t_2 \cdot F(q_1 \cdot t_1)) + C(r_{2'''},f_2)$$

$\text{COTS}_{G5} =$
$$LS(|R_1| \cdot t_1) + RA(0,t_1) + C(r_{1''},f_1) + IA(|R_2|) +$$
$$RA(0,s_2 \cdot t_2 \cdot F(s_1,t_1)) + C(r_{2'''},f_2)$$

$\text{COST}_{G6} =$
$$LS(|R_1| \cdot t_1) + RA(0,t_1) + C(r_{1''},f_1) + RA(0,t_2 \cdot F(s_1 \cdot t_1))$$
$$+ C(r_{2'''},f_2)$$

Fig. 6.7. Cost formulae

If the indexes on restriction and join attributes are clustered, the performance will be better than otherwise. The effects of indexes on the costs of query evaluation are the same in both the relational system, and GDL. Table 6.6 qualitatively shows the characteristics of the cases we evaluated. In the table, A_1 and A_2 are the attributes appearing in the restriction predicates for R_1 and R_2, respectively. In our comparison, we eliminate those algorithms which are obviously not optimal. For example, if indexes are available and effective, we select those algorithms which utilize the indexes.

Table 6.4. Characteristics of the test environments

Parameter	Test value	
b	1000	
b_l	100	
z_i	100	
z_l	100	
	R_1	R_2
$|R_i|$	10000	10000
f_i	100	100
p_i	1000	1000
e_i	1000	1000
d_{ij}	0	0
P_{ij}	1	1
P_{ji}	1	1
P_i	0.1	0.1
dd	0	0
rr	0	0
u_k	1	1

Table 6.5. Characteristics of the test cases

Parameter	Case 1		Case 2		Case 3		Case 4		Case 5	
s_i	0.001	0.01	0.001	0.01	0.1	0.1	0.1	0.1	0.0001	0.1
t_i	1	1	1	1	0.5	0.5	0.1	0.1	1	1
h_i	10	10	10	10	10	10	10	10	1	1
c_i	0	−1	−1	−1	−1	−1	0	0	0	0
c_j	0	0	0	0	−1	−1	0	0	0	0

6.3.2.1 Case 1

In case 1, there is an index on A_1 but not on A_2. The selectivity of A_1 is rather high, but that of A_2 is low. There are indexes on the join attributes. This type of query is one of the most common simple queries. An example is to retrieve enrollments for students, identified by their names, in courses which are offered in a given department.

Among applicable algorithms, we select the following as being reasonable candidates for optimality with respect to these parameter sets:

Algorithm	11/21	31/21	modified 11/11	G2
Relative cost	314	1423	144	143

Table 6.6. Characteristics of cases evaluated

	Case 1	Case 2	Case 3	Case 4	Case 5
Selectivity of A_1	High	High	Very low	Very low	Very high
Selectivity of A_2	Low	Low	Very low	Very low	Very low
Index on A_1	Yes	No	No	Yes	Yes
Index on A_2	No	No	No	Yes	Yes
Index on join attributes	Yes	Yes	No	Yes	Yes

GDL_G2 algorithm outperforms others because algorithms 11/21 and 31/21 require the scanning of the join attribute indices. Even if a real link type is not supported, GDL achieves the same cost by using the index on the join attribute of R_2. (This is a case of a virtual link type.) It is possible to obtain the same performance in the relational system, by employing the modified 11/11 algorithm. That is, after scanning the record occurrences of R_1, we get the values of the join attribute; then, we access the index of the join attribute of R_2 for these values. A similar approach is taken in SEQUEL [3].

6.3.2.2 Case 2

The only change from case 1 to case 2 is that there are no indexes on any attributes in the latter. Applicable algorithms here are limited. In the relational system, we consider 41/41 which scans R_1 and R_2 to get the record occurrences, sorts them and executes a join operation. GDL may employ G6 which scans R_1, restricts record occurrences, traverses a link type from R_1 to R_2, and executes a restriction on R_2. Estimations of the access costs are:

Algorithm	41/41	G6
Relative cost	2051	2100

We assume that a four-way sort-merge algorithm is used for sorting R_1 and R_2. The estimated cost for 41/41 is a little better than that of G6. If the link fanout is rather small, G6 performs better than 41/41; if the link fanout is large, then 41/41 is better than G6.

6.3.2.3 Case 3

This case represents the situation where the selectivities of restriction attributes are low. Since there are no indexes for these attributes, those algorithms requiring indexes are not considered.

Algorithm	41/41	G6
Relative cost	3900	3100

The result is similar to case 2.

6.3.2.4 Case 4

This represents the case that there are indexes on restriction attributes but that their selectivities are low. Note that such a situation occurs infrequently because indexes are usually constructed on highly selective attributes. Case 4 may provide, however, an approximation for the case where u_k is larger than 1.

Algorithm	31/31	G1	G3
Relative cost	642	4142	342

31/31 and G3 are essentially similar algorithms. The reason why G3 is better than 31/31 is that the number of accesses to record occurrences of R_2 is reduced in G3 due to the feedback effect from the restriction on R_1. G1 does not perform well because of the number of repeated accesses to the link files. This can be alleviated if the system is smart enough to sort pointers to avoid repetition. The estimated cost for this case is 1244. Such a phenomenon occurs for index accesses, too. Index and link access paths are not useful if there are many record occurrences to be retrieved. Scanning is better than accessing through these access paths.

6.3.2.5 Case 5

This case represents a highly selective query. An example may be retrieving the address of a given student identified by a unique key (SNO) when addresses are stored in a separate record type. The estimated costs are:

Algorithm	11/21	11/41	31/31	modified 11/11	G2
Relative cost	205	1004	1515	8	8

This case is similar to case 1. The cost differences are more significant than in case 1.

6.3.3 Semi-joins

A distinct advantage of the use of GDL real link types is the case where there exist semi-joins in a query. Suppose A_1, the set of attributes for the projection of R_1, is empty. It is not necessary to access record occurrences of R_1 if the restriction operation on R_1 can be executed only by index accesses. For example, G1 becomes:

IA
|
LA
|
IA—I—RA—RF—P

6.3.4 Three-Variable Queries

In the relational system, the cost of the execution of a three-variable query depends on how the query is decomposed. The techniques for optimal decomposition have been studied by Wong and Youssefi [76] and Blasgen and Eswaran [9] among others. In GDL, the selection of access paths among record types, i.e., the sequence of joins, is determined by the user utilizing real or virtual link types. To compare algorithms on the same basis, we assume that a given three-variable query in the relational system is decomposed into a sequence of two-variable queries that is equivalent to the path expression in GDL to be compared. Once we choose the same access path for the relational system and GDL, the costs vary in the same manner as for two-variable queries. This is true not only for three-variable queries but also for queries with more than three variables.

The query expressed in Fig. 6.8 is, for example, decomposed into two queries as in Fig. 6.9. Record type T is a temporary record type that is produced by the first query after decomposition. We assume that no indexes are constructed for the temporary record type T. We cannot use the algorithm 31 for T, because this algorithm is applicable when there are indexes on the attributes in the restriction predicate. Let us employ the algorithm 41 for T, which uses a record scan operation. The query evaluation using algorithms 31 and 41 is shown in Fig. 6.10. Also shown is the three-variable version of algorithm G1 in GDL. The cost for the evaluation of the three-variable query is the summation of the costs for these two queries. For the query and schema state characterized by the parameters shown in Table 6.7, we estimate the following costs:

1. 31/31 followed by 41/31:   855
2. GDL-G3 followed by G3:   384

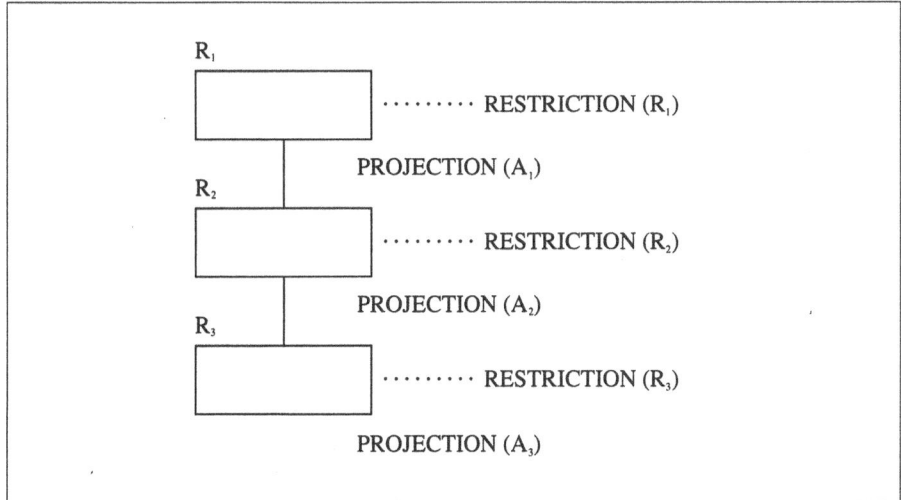

Fig. 6.8. Three-variable query

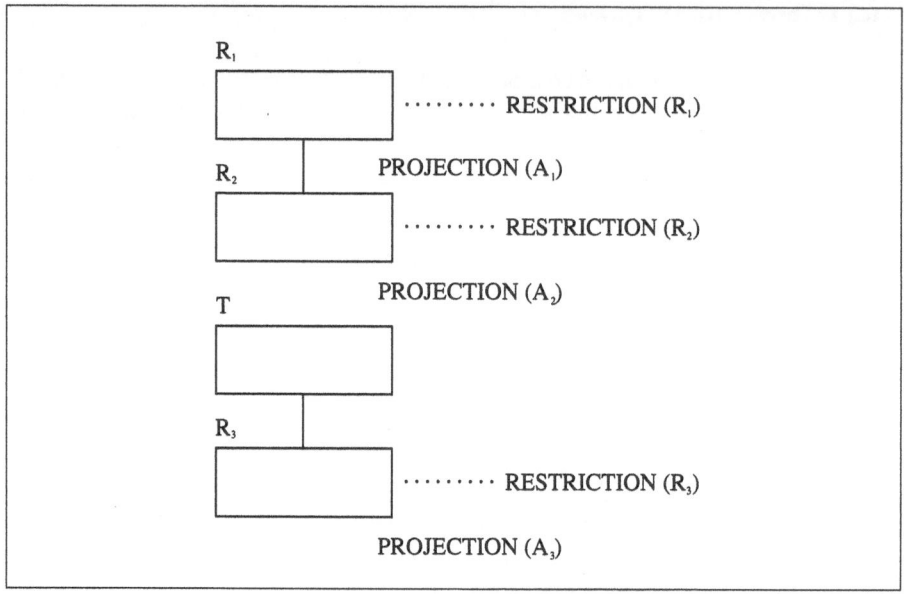

Fig. 6.9. Decomposed queries

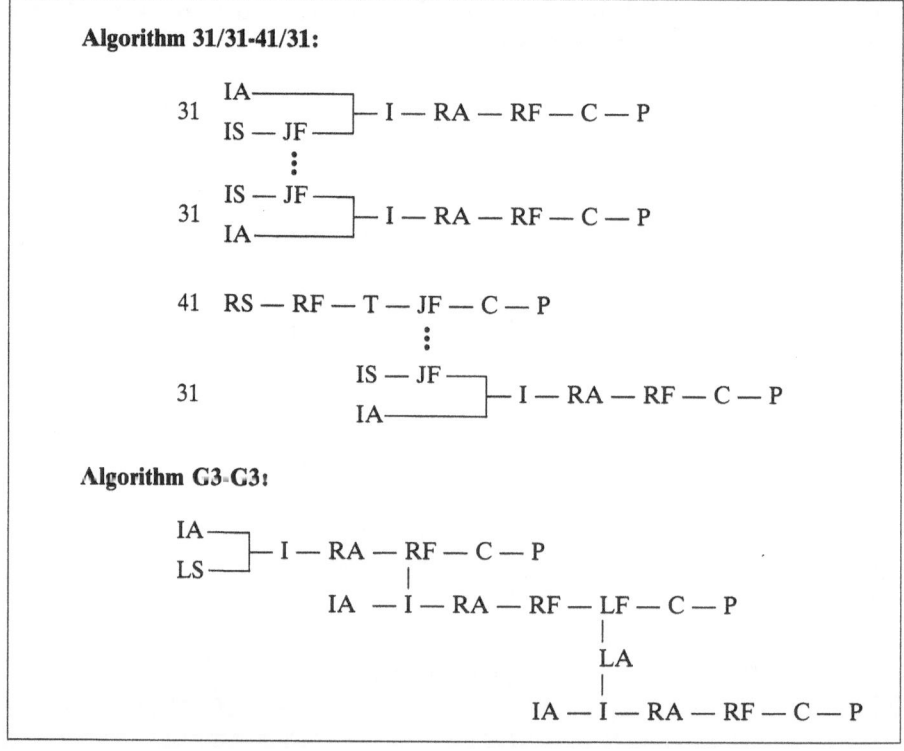

Fig. 6.10. Query evaluation algorithms for three-variable queries

Table 6.7. Characteristics of the test three-variable query and schema state

	R_1	R_2	R_3
s_i	0.1	0.1	0.1
t_i	0.1	0.1	0.1
h_i	10	10	10
c_i	0	0	0

6.4 Conclusion

The following observations are made from our case studies. Firstly, prominent differences are seen for the cases where few record occurrences are retrieved. The use of link types distinctly reduces the cost. Secondly, in the case that many record occurrences are retrieved as the response to a given query, the existence of a link type does not reduce the cost. This is because the cost for scanning files becomes comparable to, or even smaller than, the cost for using link or index access paths. Thirdly, some accesses to record occurrences can be eliminated in certain cases of semi-joins, if link types are supported. Many simple queries contain semi-joins. In practice, most queries seem to be simple; hence, the cost reduction by link access is useful.

This model does not consider the following factors:

– CPU time
– The effects of the underlying operating system such as buffer management and device scheduling

If root pages of index and link tree files are kept in core by buffering, the costs for IA and LA will be considerably reduced. This fact does not, however, significantly affect relative costs between the relational and GDM algorithms. It changes the threshold where algorithms using scanning record files, index pointer files, and link pointer files (RS, IS, LS) becomes better than ones using index/link tree files (IA, LA).

In this chapter, we concentrated on the costs of retrieval operations. The costs for storage operations are obviously higher if we have index and link storage than otherwise. Since we have not completed the implementation of GDL, we cannot quantitatively compare the time used for precompilation which executes parsing, optimization and code generation. It is, however, fair to say that GDL will be more efficient at the precompilation stage since access paths are mostly predetermined. Chamberlin et al. [14] showed that optimization of a query (one-variable and two-variable) takes several times longer than parsing and code generation in System R.

7. Conclusions

7.1 Contribution

A Graph Data Model (GDM) is proposed as a practical solution to the problems from which other data models suffer. The basic concepts developed in GDM are:

- Directed graphs as the formalizable basis for data representation structuring and operations
- Logical representation of access paths in terms of links (arcs)
- Algebraic definitions of operations on a graph including powerful link operators (operations on links)
- Concept of record lists to allow the unified manipulation of records and links during query processing

Founded on GDM, a Graph Data Language (GDL) is designed. This language demonstrates that set-at-a-time query representation in terms of operations on a graph is powerful. This is natural because a set of relations is a degenerate case of a graph. Link operators smoothly accommodate transitive closure, numerical quantifiers and grouping. Set-at-a-time query representation is also used to describe integrity constraints and views. This approach requires only minimum extension of the system in order to support these facilities in addition to the advantage of system uniformity.

By interpreting links as logical access paths, we reduce the burden on the system to determine the access paths that provide low-cost execution of data operations. The user has flexible control over performance by dynamic creation and deletion of link types. GDL requires that a query be represented as a connected graph, which makes it possible to avoid disastrous query processing. We do not mean that GDL provides an optimal execution; the efficiency still depends on the user's query formulation, but should be within an acceptable range.

Data independence, which is crucial to the ease of maintenance of data and programs, is practically achieved; a user can create and delete record types and link types even after data are loaded; operations in GDL allow the creation of any record type and any link type which can be expressed in GDL.

The scope of this book is limited to the preliminary design of GDM and GDL. Chapter 5 described the design of a prototype implementation. It proved that the implementation of GDL is rather straightforward, although GDL has to deal with two kinds of objects (records and links) while the relational model handles a single type of object (relations).

A comparison of access path strategies using an extension of Yao's cost model showed that the GDM access path strategy gives excellent performance for those queries where cardinalities of resultant record types are rather small. Since this is the case for most queries, GDM query evaluation is effective even without global query optimization. Semi-joins are also efficiently evaluated by using links.

7.2 Future Research

Since the design of GDL is at a preliminary stage, there are many areas to be investigated. Enhancements of GDL should be considered to allow aggregate and arithmetic operations, and access control. The aggregate and arithmetic operations on target record types in DML statements can be easily implemented. To allow these operations anywhere in DML statements, though conceptually simple, requires the modification of run-time procedures, specifically IRST and XRST. To design an access control feature, we need to analyze the granularity of access control. The provision of a multi-user environment requires careful design of concurrent accesses on databases.

The definitions of views and integrity controls are expressed and stored as DML statements in GDL. These are executed whenever storage operations are executed. This approach is simple and can be improved.

Parallel computation can be utilized in the design of run-time procedures to improve the response time of query processing. This is also true for the translation of DML statements into calls to run-time procedures.

A design for a graph-driven interactive query interface is useful and interesting as mentioned in Chap. 4. How easily the language can be mapped onto GDL will be one of the measures of usability of GDL in the future. Mapping of GDL to other data languages is an interesting problem. GDL can be used to implement other data models such as the relational model and the network model. It might be a powerful candidate for a conceptual schema data model in the three-level schema system [1]. The entity-relationship model [17] can be naturally mapped onto GDL. Semantic network data models [39, 59] also can be implemented on top of GDL.

Appendix A: BNF Grammar of GDL

Items enclosed by curly brackets are optional.

⟨statement⟩:: = ⟨DDL statement⟩|⟨DML statement⟩
⟨DDL statement⟩:: = ⟨define schema⟩|⟨destroy schema⟩|⟨update def⟩|
  ⟨define view⟩|⟨destroy view⟩
⟨define schema⟩:: = define schema ⟨schema name⟩ ⟨rec def list⟩ {⟨link def list⟩}
  {⟨constraint def list⟩}
⟨schema name⟩:: = ⟨identifier⟩
⟨rec def list⟩:: = ⟨rec def list⟩ ⟨record definition⟩|⟨record definition⟩
⟨record definition⟩:: = record ⟨record name⟩ ⟨attr def list⟩ {⟨clustering key
  def⟩} {⟨search key def⟩} {⟨unique key def⟩}
⟨record name⟩:: = ⟨identifier⟩
⟨attr def list⟩:: = ⟨attr def list⟩ ⟨attribute definition⟩|⟨attribute definition⟩
⟨attribute definition⟩:: = attribute ⟨attribute name⟩ ⟨attribute type⟩
⟨attribute name⟩:: = ⟨identifier⟩
⟨attribute type⟩:: = integer {⟨length⟩}|char ⟨length⟩|real {⟨length⟩, ⟨length⟩}
⟨length⟩:: = ⟨number⟩
⟨clustering key def⟩:: = clustering key ⟨key attributes⟩
⟨unique key def⟩:: = unique key ⟨key attr list⟩
⟨search key def⟩:: = search key ⟨key attr list⟩
⟨key attr list⟩:: = ⟨key attr list⟩, ⟨key attributes⟩|⟨key attributes⟩
⟨key attributes⟩:: = ⟨attribute name⟩|⟨key attributes⟩ and ⟨attribute name⟩
⟨link def list⟩:: = ⟨link def list⟩ ⟨link definition⟩|⟨link definition⟩
⟨link definition⟩:: = link ⟨link name⟩ {⟨inverse link⟩} ⟨link type def⟩
⟨inverse link⟩:: = ⟨link name⟩
⟨link type def⟩:: = ⟨real link⟩|⟨virtual link⟩
⟨real link⟩:: = ⟨node def⟩
⟨virtual link⟩:: = ⟨node def⟩ virtual ⟨attribute name⟩ ⟨comparison op⟩
  ⟨attribute name⟩
⟨comparison op⟩:: = ⟨|⟩| ≤ | ≥ | = | ≠
⟨node def⟩:: = (⟨record name⟩, ⟨record name⟩)
⟨link name⟩:: = ⟨identifier⟩
⟨constraint def list⟩:: = ⟨constraint def list⟩ ⟨constraint def⟩|⟨constraint def⟩
⟨constraint def⟩:: = ⟨rec constraint def⟩|⟨link constraint def⟩

⟨rec constraint def⟩:: = constraint record ⟨record name⟩ ⟨constraint mode⟩
    {upon ⟨operation type⟩} ⟨selection expression⟩
⟨link constraint def⟩:: = constraint link ⟨link type spec⟩ ⟨constraint mode⟩
    ⟨network expression⟩
⟨constraint mode⟩:: = never | always
⟨operation mode⟩:: = addition | deletion
⟨update def⟩:: = ⟨add def⟩ | ⟨delete def⟩ | ⟨replace def⟩ |
⟨add def⟩:: = add ⟨record definition⟩ in schema ⟨schema name⟩ {from ⟨sel
    rec⟩} | add ⟨link definition⟩ in schema ⟨schema name⟩ {from ⟨link clause⟩}
⟨delete def⟩:: = delete ⟨record name⟩ in schema ⟨schema name⟩ | delete ⟨link
    name⟩ in schema ⟨schema name⟩
⟨replace def⟩:: = replace ⟨record name⟩ in schema ⟨schema name⟩ by ⟨record
    definition⟩ {from ⟨sel rec⟩} | replace ⟨link name⟩ in schema ⟨schema name⟩ by
    ⟨link definition⟩ {from ⟨link clause⟩}
⟨define view⟩:: = define view ⟨view name⟩ on schema ⟨schema name⟩ ⟨view
    definition list⟩
⟨view definition list⟩:: = ⟨view definition list⟩ ⟨record view list⟩ {⟨link view list⟩}
⟨record view list⟩ :: = ⟨record view list⟩ ⟨record view⟩ | ⟨record view⟩
⟨link view list⟩:: = ⟨link view list⟩ ⟨link view⟩ | ⟨link view⟩
⟨record view⟩:: = record ⟨record name⟩ {(⟨attr def list⟩)} from ⟨sel rec⟩
⟨link view⟩:: = link ⟨link name⟩ {⟨node spec⟩} from ⟨link clause⟩
⟨destroy schema⟩:: = destroy schema ⟨schema name⟩
⟨destroy view⟩:: = destroy view ⟨view name⟩
⟨DML statement⟩:: = ⟨select record⟩ | ⟨select link⟩ | ⟨connect link⟩ | ⟨add re-
    cord⟩ | ⟨add link⟩ | ⟨delete record⟩ | ⟨delete link⟩ | ⟨remove record⟩ | ⟨remove
    link⟩ | ⟨replace record⟩ | ⟨reconnect link⟩ | ⟨open⟩ | ⟨close⟩ | ⟨variable declar-
    ation⟩ | ⟨sort⟩ | ⟨procedural statement⟩ | ⟨define volatile⟩
⟨define volatile⟩:: = define volatile ⟨volatile rec def⟩ | define volatile ⟨link defini-
    tion⟩
⟨volatile rec def⟩:: = record ⟨record name⟩ ⟨attr def list⟩
⟨select record⟩::= select record ⟨record name⟩:= ⟨sel rec⟩
⟨sel rec⟩::= ⟨record list⟩ {[⟨selection expression⟩]} {⟨projection spec⟩}
    {⟨sorting⟩}
⟨record list⟩::= ⟨record list⟩, ⟨record name⟩ | ⟨record name⟩
⟨projection spec⟩::= (⟨attr spec list⟩)
⟨attr spec list⟩::= ⟨attr spec list⟩, ⟨attr spec⟩ | ⟨attr spec⟩
⟨attr spec⟩::= ⟨attribute name⟩ | ⟨attribute name⟩:= ⟨attribute name⟩ |
    ⟨attribute name⟩:– ⟨rec and attr⟩ | ⟨attribute name⟩:= ⟨value⟩
⟨sorting⟩:: = sorted by ⟨record attribute list⟩
⟨record attribute list⟩:: = ⟨record attribute list⟩ ⟨record attribute name⟩ |
    ⟨rec and attr⟩
⟨selection expression⟩:: = ⟨intra record expression⟩ | ⟨network expression⟩
⟨intra record expression⟩:: = ⟨intra record expression⟩ ⟨set op⟩ ⟨intra rec
    term⟩ | ⟨intra rec term⟩
⟨set op⟩:: = + | – | ∩
⟨intra rec term⟩:: = ⟨intra rec factor⟩ | (⟨intra record expression⟩)

⟨intra rec factor⟩:: = ⟨attribute name⟩ ⟨comparison op⟩ ⟨value⟩|⟨attribute name⟩ ⟨comparison op⟩ ⟨attribute name⟩

⟨value⟩:: = a value of a defined data type|null value

⟨network expression⟩:: = ⟨network expression⟩ ⟨set op⟩ ⟨network factor⟩|⟨network factor⟩

⟨network factor⟩:: = (⟨network expression⟩)|path ⟨path expression⟩ {:⟨inter record expression⟩}

⟨path expression⟩:: = ⟨path expression⟩ ⟨linkage⟩ ⟨record clause⟩|⟨path expression⟩ ⟨linkage⟩ (⟨record clause⟩)|⟨record clause⟩ ⟨linkage⟩ ⟨record clause⟩|⟨record clause⟩ ⟨linkage⟩ (⟨record clause⟩)

⟨linkage⟩:: = ⟨existential link⟩|⟨negative existential link⟩|⟨numerical link⟩|⟨transitive link⟩

⟨existential link⟩:: = →/⟨link name*⟩/ {⟨grouping⟩} → | → {⟨grouping⟩} /⟨link name*⟩/ →

⟨negative existential link⟩:: = →/ ˜⟨link name*⟩/{⟨grouping⟩} → | → {⟨grouping⟩}/ ˜⟨link name*⟩/ →

⟨numerical link⟩:: = → {⟨grouping⟩} //⟨q⟩ ⟨link name*⟩// {⟨grouping⟩} →

⟨transitive link⟩:: = → \⟨q⟩ ⟨link name*⟩\ →

⟨link name*⟩:: = ⟨link name⟩|% ⟨link name⟩

⟨q⟩:: = {⟨comparison op⟩} ⟨num⟩

⟨num⟩:: = + |⟨number⟩

⟨number⟩:: = 1|2|3|...

⟨inter record expression⟩:: = ⟨inter record expression⟩ ⟨set op⟩ ⟨inter record term⟩|⟨inter record term⟩

⟨inter record term⟩:: = (⟨inter record expression⟩)|⟨rec and attr⟩ ⟨comparison op⟩ ⟨rec and attr⟩

⟨rec and attr⟩:: = ⟨record name⟩.⟨attribute name⟩

⟨record clause⟩:: = ⟨record name⟩|⟨record name⟩ [⟨selection expression⟩]| (⟨record name⟩ [⟨selection expression⟩])

⟨select link⟩:: = select link ⟨link name⟩:= ⟨link clause⟩

⟨link clause⟩:: = ⟨link name⟩|⟨link type spec⟩ [⟨network expression⟩]

⟨link type spec⟩:: = ⟨link name⟩|⟨link name⟩ ⟨node spec⟩

⟨node spec⟩:: = (⟨record name⟩, ⟨record name⟩)

⟨connect link⟩:: = connect link ⟨link name⟩:= (⟨record clause⟩, ⟨record clause⟩) [⟨link creation condition⟩]

⟨link creation condition⟩:: = *|⟨inter record expression⟩

⟨add record⟩:: = add record ⟨record name⟩ to ⟨record name⟩

⟨add link⟩:: = add link ⟨link name⟩ to ⟨link name⟩

⟨delete record⟩:: = delete record ⟨record name⟩ from ⟨record name⟩

⟨delete link⟩:: = delete link ⟨link name⟩ from ⟨link name⟩

⟨remove record⟩:: = remove record ⟨record clause⟩

⟨remove link⟩:: = remove link ⟨link clause⟩

⟨replace record⟩:: = replace record ⟨record clause⟩ (⟨replace attribute list⟩)

⟨replace attribute list⟩:: = ⟨replace attribute list⟩, ⟨replace attribute⟩|⟨replace attribute⟩

⟨replace attribute⟩:: = ⟨attribute name⟩:= ⟨value⟩

⟨reconnect link⟩ :: = reconnect link ⟨link clause⟩ ⟨reconnect node⟩

⟨reconnect node⟩ :: = initial node: = ⟨record clause⟩ | terminal node: = ⟨record clause⟩

⟨open⟩ :: = open schema ⟨schema name⟩ | open view ⟨view name⟩

⟨close⟩ :: = close schema ⟨schema name⟩ | close view ⟨view name⟩

⟨variable declaration⟩ :: = variable ⟨record name⟩ : ⟨record list⟩

⟨sort⟩ :: = sort ⟨record name⟩ by ⟨attr name list⟩

⟨attr name list⟩ :: = ⟨attr name list⟩ ⟨attribute name⟩ | ⟨attribute name⟩

⟨procedural statement⟩ :: = ⟨get first⟩ | ⟨get next⟩ | ⟨get previous⟩

⟨get first⟩ :: = get first ⟨record name⟩ {⟨number⟩} {⟨ordering link⟩} ⟨cursor designation⟩

⟨ordering link⟩ :: = by ⟨link name⟩

⟨cursor designation⟩ :: = with ⟨cursor name⟩

⟨cursor name⟩ :: = ⟨identifier⟩

⟨get next⟩ :: = get next {⟨number⟩} with ⟨cursor name⟩

⟨get previous⟩ :: = get previous {⟨number⟩} with ⟨cursor name⟩

Appendix B: Specification of Run-time System

This appendix describes a prototype implementation design of a GDL run-time system which consists of the following: file structures, parameters, and procedures (functions). The global data structures are described in Chap. 5.

B.1 File Structures

Each file is organized into pages. The following file structures are used in our run-time system:

1. Linear file with fixed-length records
2. B*-tree file

The occurrences of a record type are stored in a linear file, clustered by the clustering key attribute(s). Each primary key is provided with an index. Search keys are also supported by indices.

An index is implemented by a B*-tree file and a linear file. The key for the B*-tree is either a primary key attribute or a search key attribute. The second file contains URIs. Each entry in the leaf nodes of the B*-tree points to the starting location in the second file where URIs for the record occurrences containing the key value are stored.

A link type is similar in design to an index. The key for the B*-tree is a URI for the initial node. The corresponding linear file contains pairs of URIs for an initial node and a terminal node.

The URI is a page number concatenated with a unique number within the record occurrences of the same key value.

B.2 Parameters and Variables

The "i" appearing in the following parameter names denotes a number.

RTYPi   a record type—identified by a location type (a record occurrence file, a volatile record type, and a record list type) and its ID

Ri   an occurrence of RTYPi—specified by URI

LTYPi   a link type—identified by a location type (a link occur-
                 rence file, and a volatile link type) and its ID
Li   an occurrence of LTYPi
Ai   an attribute of RTYPi—identified by an offset in RTYPi
Xi   value of Ai
RSTEXP   a restriction expression
CONSTi   a constant value
RESTYP   a resultant record list type
MODE   a mode of link operators—neutral, downward or
                 upward
Q   a comparison operator used in numerical and transitive
                 link operators
DEST   a destination data structure name (volatile object name)
IDXLST   a list of indexed attributes
PRJLST   a list of pairs of a record type name and an attribute name
LNKLST   a list of link types
RECLST   a list of record types
IDX   an indexed attribute
NO   a number
BF   a name of a B*-tree file
PTR   a pointer to a record occurrence—specified by a URI
OPERAND_RLTYPi   a URI-array (designated as one of the operands or a
                 result) pointed by the i-th slot of OPERAND_
                 DISPLAY_STACK

B.3 IRST Procedure

PURPOSE   To execute an intra-record restriction
PARAMETERS   RTYP1, RSTEXP, IDXLST, RESTYP
ON ENTRY   RTYP1 is an element of OPERAND_RLTYP1. RTYP1 is
                 either in the corresponding database or in OPERAND_
                 RLTYP1.
ON EXIT   OPERAND_RLTYP1 contains the resultant record list
                 type.
ALGORITHM

                 ASGNRL;
                 if INDEX_IS_AVAILABLE *then*
                    { evaluate RSTEXP using GETIDX }
                    else
                       { GETREC;
                         evaluate RSTEXP }
                 RLPROJ;
                 /* RLPROJ takes two URI-ARRAYs (OPERAND_
                    RLTYP1 and OPERAND_RLTYP2) as operands,
                    and returns its result in OPERAND_RLTYP1.
                    */

CALLED FROM   MAIN
CALLS   ASGNRL, GETIDX, GETREC, RLPROJ

B.4 XRST Procedure

PURPOSE   To execute an inter-record restriction
PARAMETERS   RTYP1, RTYP2, RSTEXP, RESTYP
ON ENTRY   RTYP1 and RTYP2 are elements of OPERAND_RLTYP1.
ON EXIT   OPERAND_RLTYP1 contains the resultant record list type.
ALGORITHM
        for RTYP1_DO_GETREC;
        for RTYP2_DO_GETREC;
        ASGNRL;
        for each occurrence of OPERAND_RLTYP1 *do*
          { evaluate RSTEXP };
        RLPROJ;
CALLED FROM   MAIN
CALLS   ASGNRL, GETREC, RLPROJ

B.5 EXT Procedure

PURPOSE   To execute an existential link operator
PARAMETERS   LTYP1, RTYP1, RTYP2, MODE, Ai, RESTYP
ON ENTRY   RTYP1 is an element of OPERAND_RLTYP1. LTYP1 is defined as a link type from RTYP1 to RTYP2. Ai specifies a grouping on either node which is determined by MODE. It can be null.
ON EXIT   OPERAND_RLTYP1 contains the resultant record list type.
ALGORITHM
        GETLNK into OPERAND_RLTYP2;
        if GROUPING_EXISTS *then*
          { PUSH; GETIDX; UNI; POP };
        UNI; POP;
        RLPROJ;
CALLED FROM   MAIN
CALLS   GETLNK, GETIDX, PUSH, RLPROJ, POP, UNI

B.6 NEGEXT Procedure

PURPOSE   To execute a negative existential link operator
PARAMETERS   LTYP1, RTYP1, RTYP2, MODE, Ai, RESTYP

ON ENTRY   RTYP1 is an element of OPERAND_RLTYP1. LTYP1 is
                    defined as a link type from RTYP1 to RTYP2. Ai specifies
                    a grouping on either node which is determined by MODE. It
                    can be null.
ON EXIT   OPERAND_RLTYP1 contains the resultant record list
                    type.
ALGORITHM

                    ASGNRL;
                    copy RTYP1 or RTYP2 to OPERAND_RLTYP2
                        depending on MODE;
                    PUSH;
                    GETLNK into OPERAND_RLTYP2;
                    if GROUPING_EXISTS then
                        { PUSH; GETIDX; UNI; POP };
                    DIF; POP;
                    RLPROJ;
CALLED FROM   MAIN
CALLS   ASGNRL, GETLNK, GETIDX, RLPROJ, DIF, PUSH,
                    POP, UNI

B.7 NUM Procedure

PURPOSE   To execute a numerical link operator
PARAMETERS   LTYP1, RTYP1, RTYP2, A1, A2, MODE, RTYP, Q
ON ENTRY   LTYP1 is defined as (RTYP1, RTYP2). RTYP1 is an element
                    of OPERAND_RLTYP1. A1 and A2 specify groupings. A1 is
                    an attribute of RTYP1 and A2 is an attribute of RTYP2. A1
                    and A2 can be null.
ON EXIT   OPERAND_RLTYP1 contains the resultant record list
                    type.
ALGORITHM

                    if GROUPING_EXISTS_ON_RTYP1 then do
                        { GROUP;
                          for each group do SORT };
                    if GROUPING_EXISTS_ON_RTYP2 then do
                        { GROUP;
                          for each group do SORT };
                    for each group of RTYP1 do
                        { GETLNK to TEMP;
                          check the number of link occurrences };
                    ASGNRL;
                    store the result to OPERAND_RLTYP1;
                    RLPROJ;
CALLED FROM   MAIN
CALLS   ASGNRL, GROUP, SORT, GETLNK, RLPROJ

B.8 TRN Procedure

PURPOSE	To execute a transitive link operator
PARAMETERS	LTYP1, RTYP1, MODE, Q
ON ENTRY	LTYP1 is a recursive link type. RTYP1 is an element of OPERAND_RLTYP1.
ON EXIT	The resultant record list type is in OPERAND-RLTYP1.
ALGORITHM	

/* If Q is " $\leq$ n" */
ASGNRL;
for N times do GETLNK;
RLPROJ;
/* Similar in the other cases */

CALLED FROM	MAIN
CALLS	ASGNRL, GETLNK, RLPROJ

B.9 LNKCRT Procedure

PURPOSE	To execute a link creation operation between two record types
PARAMETERS	RTYP1, RTYP2, RSTEXP
ON ENTRY	RSTEXP can be null. In this case, a Cartesian product will be constructed between two record types.
ON EXIT	A link type from RTYP1 to RTYP2 is constructed in OPERAND_RLTYP1.
ALGORITHM	

for RTYP1_DO_GETREC;
for RTYP2_DO_GETREC;
ASGNRL;
for all combinations of R1 *in* RTYP1 *and*
   R2 *in* RTYP2 *do* evaluate RSTEXP;
DELRL;

CALLED FROM	MAIN
CALLS	ASGNRL, GETREC, DELRL

B.10 PROJ Procedure

PURPOSE	To execute a projection from a current record list type
PARAMETERS	PRJLST, DEST
ON ENTRY	PRJLST may involve more than one record type.
ON EXIT	DEST contains the occurrences of a new record type specified.
ALGORITHM	

GETREC into DEST;
for each occurrence of OPERAND_RLTYP1
   do copy values of attributes specified by PRJLST into
      DEST;

CALLED FROM   MAIN
CALLS   GETREC

B.11 FETCH Procedure

PURPOSE   To retrieve the occurrences of a given record type—a degen-
               erated case of a projection
PARAMETERS   DEST
ON ENTRY   The source is in OPERAND_RLTYP1
ON EXIT   DEST contains the values of a specified record type.
ALGORITHM
               GETREC into DEST;
CALLED FROM   MAIN
CALLS   GETREC

B.12 UNI, INTS, DIF Procedures

PURPOSE   To execute a set operation (union, intersection, and
               difference)
PARAMETERS   none
ON ENTRY   OPERAND_RLTYP1 and OPERAND_RLTYP2 contain
               operands.
ON EXIT   OPERAND_RLTYP1 contains the resultant record list
               type.
ALGORITHM
               ASGNRL;
               perform the set operation;
               /* The result is in OPERAND_RLTYP3. */
               DELRL(2);
               /* OPERAND_RLTYP3 becomes
                   OPERAND_RLTYP1. */
CALLED FROM   MAIN, EXT, NEGEXT
CALLS   ASGNRL, DELRL

B.13 RADD Procedure

PURPOSE   To add record occurrences
PARAMETERS   RTYP1, RTYP2, IDXLST
ON ENTRY   RTYP1 and RTYP2 must be compatible. RTYP1 is a
               volatile record type and RTYP2 is a resident record type.
ON EXIT   The occurrences of RTYP1 are added to RTYP2. The search
               keys (indexes), if any, are added to the index files.
ALGORITHM
               for each occurrence of RTYP1 *do*
                   { ADDREC;
                   for each element of IDXLST *do*
                   ADDIDX };

CALLED FROM   MAIN
CALLS   ADDREC, ADDIDX

B.14 RDEL Procedure

PURPOSE   To delete record occurrences and the associated indexes and link occurrences

PARAMETERS   RTYP1, RTYP2, IDXLST, LNKLST

ON ENTRY   RTYP1 is compatible with RTYP2. RTYP1 is a volatile record type. RTYP2 is a resident record type.

ON EXIT   The occurrences of RTYP1 are deleted from RTYP2. The link occurrences incident with the occurrences of RTYP1 are deleted. The indexes for RTYP2, if any, are also updated.

ALGORITHM

for each occurrence of RTYP1 *do*
    { DELREC;
       for each element of IDXLST *do*
          DELIDX;
       for each element of LNKLST *do*
          DELLNK };

CALLED FROM   MAIN
CALLS   DELREC, DELIDX, DELLNK

B.15 LADD Procedure

PURPOSE   To add link occurrences

PARAMETERS   LTYP1, LTYP2

ON ENTRY   LTYP1 must be compatible with LTYP2. LTYP1 is a volatile link type. LTYP2 is a resident link type. The incident record occurrences must exist as resident.

ON EXIT   The occurrences of LTYP1 are added to LTYP2.

ALGORITHM

for each occurrence of LTYP1 *do*
    ADDLNK;

CALLED FROM   MAIN
CALLS   ADDLNK

B.16 LDEL Procedure

PURPOSE   To delete link occurrences

PARAMETERS   LTYP1, LTYP2

ON ENTRY   LTYP1 is compatible with LTYP2. LTYP1 is a volatile link type. LTYP2 is a resident record type.

ON EXIT   The occurrences of LTYP1 are deleted from LTYP2.

ALGORITHM

    for each occurrence of LTYP1
    do DELLNK;
CALLED FROM MAIN
CALLS   DELLNK

B.17 PUSH Procedure

PURPOSE   To execute a push operation on the URI_STACK.
PARAMETERS none
ON ENTRY   The operand is in OPERAND_RLTYP1.
ON EXIT   OPERAND_RLTYP1 is pushed onto the URI_STACK.
ALGORITHM

    push OPERAND_RLTYP1 to URI_STACK; DELRL;
CALLED FROM MAIN, EXT, NEGEXT
CALLS   DELRL

B.18 POP Procedure

PURPOSE   To execute a pop operation.
PARAMETERS none
ON ENTRY   The URI_STACK should not be empty.
ON EXIT   The top of the URI_STACK is moved to
        OPERAND_RLTYP1.
ALGORITHM

    ASGNRL;
    pop the URI_ARRAY at the top of URI_STACK to
    OPERAND_RLTYP1;
CALLED FROM MAIN, NEGEXT
CALLS   ASGNRL

B.19 RLPROJ Procedure

PURPOSE   To execute a record list projection
PARAMETERS RECLST
ON ENTRY   RECLST is a specification of which elements are to be projec-
        ted. OPERAND_RLTYP1 and OPERAND_RLTYP2
        contain the operands.
ON EXIT   OPERAND_RLTYP1 contains the resultant record list
        type.
ALGORITHM

    ASGNRL;
    for each occurrence of OPERAND_RLTYP2 *do*
     for each element of RECLST *do*
       copy corresponding URI into
         OPERAND_RLTYP3;
    DELRL(2);

| CALLED FROM | IRST, XRST, EXT, NEGEXT, NUM, TRN, NTRN |
| CALLS | ASGNRL, DELRL |

B.20 GETREC Procedure

PURPOSE	To get record occurrences into a working area
PARAMETERS	RTYP1, DEST
ON ENTRY	
ON EXIT	DEST contains the occurrences of RTYP1.
ALGORITHM	

> *if* DEST_IS_NULL *then* ASGNREC;
> /* In this case, a RECORD_ARRAY newly allocated is
>   the destination. */
> *if* RTYP1_IN_RECORD_STACK *then*
>   { *for each occurrence of* RTYP1
>   *do* { copy it to DEST }}
>   *else*
>   { *for each occurrence of* RTYP1
>   *do* { SRCHTRE; copy it to DEST }};

| CALLED FROM | IRST, XRST, LNKCRT, PROJ, FETCH, GROUP |
| CALLS | SRCHTRE |

B.21 GETIDX Procedure

PURPOSE	To get indices (URIs) of given values(s)
PARAMETERS	IDX, CONST1, CONST2, DEST
ON ENTRY	CONST1 and CONST2 must be in the domain of IDX. If CONST2 is not null, then a range search will be executed.
ON EXIT	The result is stored in DEST.
ALGORITHM	

> *if* DEST_IS_NULL *then* ASGNRL;
> /* In this case, a RECORD_ARRAY newly allocated is the
>   destination. */
> *if* CONST2_IS_NULL *then* SRCHTRE
>   *else*
>   { *for* CONST1 *to* CONST2 *do* SRCHTRE };

| CALLED FROM | IRST, GROUP, EXT, NEGEXT |
| CALLS | ASGNRL, SRCHTRE |

B.22 GETLNK Procedure

PURPOSE	To get link occurrences for given initial node(s)
PARAMETERS	LTYP1, RTYP1, DEST
ON ENTRY	RTYP1 is the initial node of LTYP.
ON EXIT	DEST contains the result.

ALGORITHM

> *if* DEST_IS_NULL *then* ASGNRL;
> *for each occurrence of* RTYP1 *do*
>   { SRCHTRE; copy values to DEST };

CALLED FROM   EXT, NEGEXT, NUM, TRN
CALLS   ASGNRL, SRCHTRE

B.23 GROUP Procedure

PURPOSE   To group a record type
PARAMETERS   RTYP1, A1
ON ENTRY   A1 is an attribute of RTYP1.
ON EXIT   RTYP1 is grouped by the value of A1.
ALGORITHM

> *if* A1_IS_INDEXED *then*
>   { group occurrences using GETIDX }
>   *else*
>   { GETREC; SORT; group them };

CALLED FROM   NUM, TRN
CALLS   ASGNREC, GETIDX, GETREC, SORT

B.24 SORT Procedure

PURPOSE   To sort a record type
PARAMETERS   RTYP1, A1
ON ENTRY   A1 is an attribute of RTYP1.
ON EXIT   RTYP1 is sorted by the value of A1.
ALGORITHM

> sort RTYP1 by A1;

CALLED FROM   GROUP, MAIN
CALLS   none

B.25 ASGNRL Procedure

PURPOSE   To assign a location for storage of OPERAND_RLTYP1.
PARAMETERS   none
ON ENTRY   At least one of the URI_STACKs has unused space.
ON EXIT   A URI_ARRAY is allocated for storage of record list type
               (OPERAND_RLTYPi).

ALGORITHM

> find the URI_STACK which does not contain
> OPERAND_RLTYPi and has the smallest used space;
> update OPERAND_DISPLAY_STACK;

CALLED FROM   LNKCRT, RLPROJ, GETIDX, GETLNK, IRST,
               XRST, NEGEXT, NUM, TRN, UNI, INTS, DIF, POP
CALLS   none

B.26 DELRL Procedure

PURPOSE	To delete a given number of OPERAND_RLTYPs.
PARAMETERS	NO
ON ENTRY	NO contains the number of URI-ARRAYs (OPERAND_RLTYPs) to be deleted.
ON EXIT	OPERAND_DISPLAY_STACK is updated.
ALGORITHM	
	delete a given number (NO) of entries from OPERAND _DISPLAY_STACK;
CALLED FROM	UNI, INTS, DIF, RLPROJ, PUSH, LNKCRT
CALLS	none

B.27 ASGNREC Procedure

PURPOSE	To assign a RECORD_STACK to a given record type
PARAMETERS	none
ON ENTRY	
ON EXIT	The RECORD_STACK that has the smallest used space is assigned to storage of a record type.
ALGORITHM	
	If the RECORD_ARRAY pointed by the top element of RECORD_DISPLAY_STACK is not useful, then discard it;
	if { there is unused space in either RECORD_STACK } *then*
	{ allocate the one with more unused space }
	else
	{ overwrite circularly };
	update RECORD_DISPLAY_STACK;
CALLED FROM	GETREC
CALLS	none

B.28 ADDREC Procedure

PURPOSE	To add a record occurrence into a database
PARAMETERS	RTYP1, R1, IDXLST
ON ENTRY	R1 is an occurrence of RTYP1.
ON EXIT	R1 is added to RTYP1. Its indexes are updated.
ALGORITHM	
	NOOFREC := SRCHTRE;
	determine a URI for R1;
	store R1 with the URI in the sequential file;
	put the pointer in the B*-tree;
	for each INDEX *do* ADDIDX;
CALLED FROM	RADD

CALLS   SRCHTRE, ADDIDX

B.29 DELREC Procedure

PURPOSE   To delete a record occurrence
PARAMETERS   RTYP1, R1, IDXLST, LNKLST
ON ENTRY   R1 is an occurrence of RTYP1.
ON EXIT   R1 is deleted from RTYP1. Its indexes are deleted. The link
                    occurrences incident with R1 are also deleted.
ALGORITHM

                    DELTRE;
                    for each element of IDXLST *do* DELIDX;
                    for each element of LNKLST *do*
                         { *if* SRCHTRE $\neq$ 0 *then* DELLNK }
CALLED FROM   RDEL
CALLS   DELTRE, DELIDX, DELLNK, SRCHTRE

B.30 ADDIDX Procedure

PURPOSE   To add a pointer to R1 in an index file
PARAMETERS   IDX, R1
ON ENTRY   IDX is an index of the record type which R1 belongs to.
ON EXIT   The pointer to R1 is added to IDX.
ALGORITHM

                    compute the value V of IDX for R1;
                    if SRCHTRE = 0 *then* ADDTRE
                      else { add it to the linear file };
CALLED FROM   ADDREC
CALLS   ADDTRE, SRCHTRE

B.31 DELIDX Procedure

PURPOSE   To delete an index
PARAMETERS   IDX, R1
ON ENTRY   IDX is an index file of the record type which R1 belongs to.
ON EXIT   The pointer to R1 is deleted from IDX.
ALGORITHM

                    compute the value V of IDX for R1;
                    if SRCHTRE = 1 *then*
                        { DELETE with V and URI of R1 }
                        else
                        { delete R1 from the linear file };
CALLED FROM   RDEL
CALLS   DELTRE

B.32 ADDLNK Procedure

PURPOSE   To add a link occurrence
PARAMETERS   LTYP1, R1, R2
ON ENTRY   (R1, R2) is in the domain of LTYP.
ON EXIT   (R1, R2) is added to LTYP.
ALGORITHM

> *if* SRCHTRE (LTYP, R1) $\neq$ 0 *then*
> { add R1 in the linear file }
> *else* ADDTRE (LTYP, R1, R2);

CALLED FROM   LADD
CALLS   SRCHTRE, ADDTRE

B.33 DELLNK Procedure

PURPOSE   To delete a link occurrence
PARAMETERS   LTYP1, R1, R2
ON ENTRY   (R1, R2) is in the domain of LTYP.
ON EXIT   The link occurrence (R1, R2) is deleted from LTYP.
ALGORITHM

> *if* SRCHTRE(LTYP, R1) = 0 *then* ERROR
> *else*
> { *if* R2_IS_NULL *then* DELTRE(LTYP, R1)
> *else* { delete R2 from the linear list }
> };

CALLED FROM   LDEL, RDEL
CALLS   SRCHTRE, DELTRE

B.34 SRCHTRE Function

PURPOSE   To search a B*-tree
PARAMETERS   BF, X, PTR
ON ENTRY   X is a value to be searched in BF.
ON EXIT   If X is found in BF then the value of this function is the
                number of pointers to record occurrences (URIs).
                Otherwise, it is 0. PTR contains the first pointer.
ALGORITHM
                search the tree from the root until X is found or the tree is
                exhausted;
CALLED FROM   GETREC, GETIDX, GETLNK, ADDREC, ADDIDX,
                ADDLNK, DELREC, DELIDX, DELLNK
CALLS   none

B.35 ADDTRE Procedure

PURPOSE   To add a pointer to a B*-tree

PARAMETERS   BF, X1, PTR
ON ENTRY   X1 is a key value of the B*-tree BF. PTR is a pointer to be
                   stored in BF.
ON EXIT   PTR is stored in BF.
ALGORITHM

                   make a new entry of X1 with PTR in BF;
CALLED FROM   ADDREC, ADDIDX, ADDLNK
CALLS   none

B.36 DELTRE Procedure

PURPOSE   To delete an item from a B*-tree
PARAMETERS   BF, X1
ON ENTRY   The entry of X1 must exit in BF.
ON EXIT   PTR with X1 is deleted from BF.
ALGORITHM

                   delete an entry of X1 from BF;
CALLED FROM   DELREC, DELIDX, DELLNK
CALLS   none

Bibliography[1]

1. ANSI/X3/SPARC Study Group on Database Management Systems (1975) Interim report. Technical Report, ANSI, Feb 1975. Edited version (1978) Inf. Syst. 3(3): 173–191
2. Astrahan MM, Chamberlin DD (1975) Implementation of a structured English query language. Commun. ACM, Oct 1975, 18(10): 580–588
3. Astrahan MM, Blasgen MW, Chamberlin DD, Eswaran KP, Gray JN, Griffiths PP, King WF, Lorie RA, McJones PR, Mehl JW, Putzolu GR, Traiger IL, Wade BW, Watson V (1976) System R: relational approach to database management. ACM Trans. Database Syst., June 1976, 1(2): 97–137
4. Astrahan MM, Kim W (1980) Performance of the System R access path selection mechanism. In: Information processing 80, IFIP, pp 487–491
5. Babb E (1979) Implementing a relational database by means of specified hardware. ACM Trans. Database Syst., Mar 1979, 4(1): 1–29
*6. Bachman CW (1969) Data structure diagrams. ACM Database, 1(2): 4–10
*7. Bayer R, McCreight EM (1972) Organization and maintenance of large ordered indices. Acta Inf., 1(3): 173–189
8. Bernstein PA, Chiu DM (1981) Using semi-joins to solve relational queries. J. ACM, 28(1)
9. Blasgen MW, Eswaran KP (1976) On the evaluation of queries in a relational data base system. Technical Report RJ1745, IBM Research Report, Apr 1976
10. Blasgen MW, Eswaran KP (1977) Storage and access in relational data bases. IBM Syst. J., 16(4): 363–377
11. Bradley J (1978) An extended owner-coupled set data model. ACM Trans. Database Syst., Dec 1978, 3(4): 385–416
*12. Browne JC, Kunii TL, Kunii HS, Takahashi K, Katayama O, Oyanagi K (1980) An evolutionary data base management system. In: Proc. IEEE COMPSAC 80, IEEE, Oct 1980, pp 320–326
13. Chamberlin DD, Astrahan MM, Eswaran KP, Griffiths PP, Lorie RA, Mehl JW, Reisner P, Wade BW (1976) SEQUEL 2: a unified approach to data definition, manipulation and control. IBM J. Res. Dev., 20(6): 560–575
14. Chamberlin DD, Astrahan MM, King WF, Lorie RA, Mehl JW, Price TG, Schkolnick M, Griffiths Selinger P, Slutz DR, Wade BW, Yost RA (1981) Support for repetitive transactions and ad hoc queries in System R. ACM Trans. Database Syst., Mar 1981, 6(1): 70–94
*15. Chamberlin DD, Astrahan MM, Blasgen MW, Gray JN, King WF, Lindsay BG, Lorie R, Mehl JW, Price TG, Putzolu F, Griffiths Selinger P, Schkolnick M, Slutz DR, Traiger IL, Wade BW, Yost RA (1981) A history and evaluation of System R. Commun. ACM, Oct 1981, 24(10): 632–646
*16. Chan A, Danberg S, Fox S, Lin W-TK, Nori A, Ries D (1982) Storage and access

---

[1] Titles that are preceded with an asterisk (*) are not referred to in the text.

structures to support a semantic data model. In: Proc. 8th Int. Conf. on Very Large Data Bases, The VLDB Endowment, May 1982, pp 122–130

17. Chen PPS (1976) The Entity-Relationship Model—toward a unified view of data. ACM Trans. Database Syst., Mar 1976, 1(1): 9–36

*18. Chen PP, Yao SB (1977) Design and performance tools for data base systems. In: Proc. 3rd Int. Conf. On Very Large Data Bases, IEEE, pp 222–234

19. Codd EF (1970) A relational model of data for large shared data banks. Commun. ACM, Jun 1970, 13(6): 377–387

20. Codd EF (1972) Relational completeness of data base sublanguages. In: Rustin R(ed) Data base systems. Prentice-Hall, Englewood Cliffs NJ, pp 65–98 (Courant Computer Science Symposia Series, Vol 6)

*21. Date CJ (1975) An introduction to database systems. Addison Wesley, Reading MA

22. Date CJ (1980) An introduction to the Unified Database Language (UDL). In: Proc. 6th Int. Conf. on Very Large Data Bases, IEEE/ACM, pp 15–32

*23. Date CJ (1983) An introduction to database systems. Addison Wesley, Reading MA

24. Dayal U (1979) Schema-mapping problems in database systems. PhD thesis, Harvard University, Aug 1979

25. Dayal U, Bernstein P (1982) On the updatability of network views—extending relational view theory to the network model. Inf. Syst., 7(1): 29–46

26. Dayal U, Goodman N (1982) Query optimization for CODASYL database systems. In: Proc. Int. Conf. on Management of Data, ACM-SIGMOD, pp 138–150

27. Data Base Task Group of CODASYL Programming Language Committee (1971) Final Report. Technical Report, CODASYL, Apr 1971

*28. Deo N (1974) Graph theory with applications to engineering and computer science. Prentice-Hall, Englewood Cliffs NJ

*29. Elliott L, Kunii HS, Browne JC (1978) A data management system for engineering and scientific computing. In: Proc. Conf. on Scientific and Engineering Data Management. May 1978

30. Elmasri R, Wiederhold G (1981) GORDAS: a formal high-level language for the entity-relationship model. In: Entity-Relationship Approach to Information Modeling and Analysis. ER Institute, pp 49–72. (Also available from North-Holland)

31. Epstein R, Hawthorn R (1980) Design decisions for the intelligent database machine. In: Proc. AFIPS NCC. AFIPS, May 1980, pp 237–241

32. Finkelstein S (1982) Common expression analysis in database applications. In: Proc. Int. Conf. on Management of Data. ACM-SIGMOD, pp 235–245

*33. Fujishiro I, Shirai Y, Kunii HS, Kunii TL (1987) Extending external views on a link-oriented data model. In: Proc. IEEE 11th Int. COMPSAC. IEEE, Oct 1987, pp 397–403

34. Furtado AL, Kerschberg L (1977) An Algebra of Quotient Relations. In: Proc. Int. Conf. on Management of Data. ACM-SIGMOD, Toronto, Aug 1977, pp 1–8

35. Gotlieb L (1975) Computing joins of relations. In: Proc. Int. Conf. on Management of Data. ACM-SIGMOD, May 1975, pp 55–63

36. Gray JN, Lorie RA, Putzolu GR, Traiger IL (1976) Granularity of locks and degrees of consistency in a shared data base. In: Modelling in Data Base Management Systems, North-Holland, pp 365–394

*37. Gray JN (1979) Notes on data base operating systems. In: Operating systems. Springer-Verlag

*38. Hawthorn P, Stonebraker M (1979) Performance analysis of a relational data base management system. In: Proc. Int. Conf. on Management of Data. ACM-SIGMOD, pp 1–12

39. Hendrix GG (1977) Some general comments on sematic networks. In: Proc. 5th Int. Joint Conf. on Artificial Intelligence, pp 984–985

40. Horowitz E, Sahni S (1976) Fundamentals of data structures. Computer Science Press, Potomac MD

*41. Hudyma R, Kornatowski J, Ladd I (1980) Implementing a micro-computer database management system. Technical Report, Computer Systems Research Group, Univ. of Toronto, Toronto, Ontario

*42. IMS/VS general information manual (1975) IBM, White Plains NY, GH20-1260-3

*43. Inmon WH (1981) Effective data base design. Prentice-Hall, Englewood Cliffs NJ

44. Jacobs BR (1982) On database logic. ACM Trans. Database Syst., 29(2): 310–332

*45. Kedem Z, Mohan C, Silberschatz A (1982) An efficient deadlock removal scheme for non-two-phase locking protocols. In: Proc. 8th Int. Conf. on Very Large Data Bases, IEEE, Sep 1982, pp 91–97

46. Kim W (1982) On optimizing an SQL-like nested query. ACM Trans. Database Syst., Sep 1982, 7(3): 443–469

47. Knuth D (1973) The art of computer programming. Addison-Wesley, Reading MA

*48. Kornatowski JZ (1979) The MRS users manual. Computer Systems Research Group, Univ. of Toronto, Toronto, Ontario

*49. Kunii HS (1987) DBMS with Graph Data Model for knowledge handling. In: Proc. FJCC. IEEE, Oct. 1987, pp 138–142

*50. Kunii TL, Kunii HS (1977) Design criteria for distributed database systems. In: Proc. 3rd Int. Conf. on Very Large Data Bases. Tokyo, Oct 1977

*51. Kunii TL, Kunii HS (1977) Database design. In: Proc. 10th Hawaiian Int. Conf. on System Sciences. Jan 1977

*52. Kunii TL, Browne JC, Kunii HS (1978) An architecture for evolutionary database system design. In: Proc. IEEE 2nd Int. COMPSAC. IEEE, Nov 1978

*53. Kunii TL, Kunii HS (1979) Architecture of a virtual graphic database system for interactive CAD. Computer-Aided Design, May 1979, 11(3): 132–135

54. Manola F, Pirotte A (1982) CQLF—a query language for CODASYL-type databases. In: Proc. Int. Conf. on Management of Data. ACM-SIGMOD, pp 94–103

*55. Olle TW (1977) The codasyl approach to data base management. John Wiley & Sons

56. Ozkarahan EA, Schuster SA, Smith KC (1975) RAP—an associative processor for data base management. In: Proc. NCC, AFIPS, pp 379–387

57. Rosenthal R, Reiner D (1982) An architecture for query optimization. In: Proc. Int. Conf. on Management of Data. ACM-SIGMOD, pp 246–255

58. Rothnie JB (1975) Evaluating inter-entry retrieval expressions in a relational data base management system. In: Proc. AFIPS NCC. AFIPS, pp 417–423

59. Roussopoulos N (1975) A semantic network model for data bases. PhD thesis, Dept. of Comput. Sci., Univ. of Toronto, Toronto, Ontario

*60. Rustin R (ed) (1974) Proc. ACM-SIGFIDET debate: data models: data-structure set versus relational. ACM, Ann Arbor

61. Schkolnick M (1977) A clustering algorithm for hierarchical structures. ACM Trans. Database Syst., Mar 1977, 2(1): 27–44

62. Selinger PG, Astrahan MM, Chamberlin DD, Lorie RA, Price TG (1979) Access path selection in a relational database management system. In: Proc. Int. Conf. on Management of Data. ACM, pp 23–34

*63. Severance DG (1975) A parametric model of alternative file structures. Inf. Syst., 2(1): 51–55

64. Shipman DW (1979) The functional data model and the data language DAPLEX. In: Proc. Int. Conf. on Management of Data. ACM-SIGMOD, May 1979, pp 1–19

65. Schneiderman B, Thomas G (1980) Path expressions for complex queries and automatic database program conversion. In: Proc. 6th Int. Conf. on Very Large Data Bases. IEEE/ACM, pp 33–44

*66. Shu NC, Housel BC, Taylor RW, Ghosh SP, Lum VY (1977) EXPRESS: a data EXtraction, Processing and REStructuring System. ACM Trans. Database Syst., Jun 1977, 2(2): 134–177

*67. Smith JM, Chang PY (1975) Optimizing the performance of a relational algebra database interface. Commun. ACM, Oct 1975, 18(10): 568–579

*68. Smith JM, Smith DCP (1977) Database abstractions: aggregation and generalization. ACM Trans. Database Syst., Jun 1977, 2(2): 105–133

69. Stonebraker M, Wong E, Kreps P (1976) The design and implementation of INGRES. ACM Trans. Database Syst., Sep 1976, 1(3): 189–222

*70. Taylor RW, Frank RL (1976) CODASYL data base management systems. Comput. Surv., Mar 1976 8(1): 67–104

*71. Teorey TJ, Fry FP (1982) Design of database structures. Prentice-Hall, Englewood Cliffs NJ

  72. Tsichritzis D (1976) LSL: a link and selector language. In: Proc. Int. Conf. on Management of Data. ACM-SIGMOD, Washington DC, Jun 1976, pp 123–133

*73. Tsichritzis DC, Lochovsky FH (1976) Hierarchical data base management. Comput. Surv., Mar 1976 8(1): 105–124

*74. Tsichritzis DC, Lochovsky FH (1981) Data models. Prentice-Hall, Englewood Cliffs NJ

*75. Wirth N (1975) On the design of programming languages. In: Proc. 1st Int. Conf. on Software Engineering. IEEE/ACM pp 386–393

  76. Wong E, Youssefi KAA (1976) Decomposition—a strategy for query processing. ACM Trans. Database Syst., 1(3): 223–241

*77. Yamaguchi K, Merten AG (1974) Methodology for transferring programs and data. In: Proc. Int. Conf. on Management of Data. ACM-SIGMOD, pp 141–155

  78. Yao SB (1977) An attributebased model for database access cost analysis. ACM Trans. Database Syst., Mar 1977, 2(1): 45–67

  79. Yao SB (1978) Optimization of query evaluation algorithms. Technical Report TR283, Comput. Sci. Dept., Purdue University, Aug 1978

  80. Yao SB (1979) Optimization of query evaluation algorithms. ACM Trans. Database Syst., Jun 1979, 4(2): 133–155

  81. Youssefi K, Wong E (1979) Query processing in a relational database management system. In: Proc. 5th Int. Conf. on Very Large Data Bases. IEEE, pp 409–417

  82. Zloof MM (1975) Query by Example. In: Proc. AFIPS NCC, ACM, pp 431–438

Symbols and Abbreviations

Subject Index